A

A

With expert readings and forecasts, you can chart a course to romance, adventure, good health, or career opportunities while gaining valuable insight into yourself and others. Offering a daily outlook for 18 full months, this fascinating guide shows you:

- The important dates in your life
- What to expect from an astrological reading
- How the stars can help you stay healthy and fit
  And more!

Let this sound advice guide you through a year of heavenly possibilities—for today and for every day of 2013!

SYDNEY OMARR'S® DAY-BY-DAY ASTROLOGICAL GUIDE FOR

ARIES—March 21–April 19
TAURUS—April 20–May 20
GEMINI—May 21–June 20
CANCER—June 21–July 22
LEO—July 23–August 22
VIRGO—August 23–September 22
LIBRA—September 23–October 22
SCORPIO—October 23–November 21
SAGITTARIUS—November 22–December 21
CAPRICORN—December 22–January 19
AQUARIUS—January 20–February 18
PISCES—February 19–March 20

IN 2013

2013
— A BRAND-NEW YEAR —
PROMISING NEW START

Sydney Omarr's®

DAY-BY-DAY ASTROLOGICAL GUIDE FOR

LIBRA

SEPTEMBER 23–OCTOBER 22

2013

by Trish MacGregor
with Rob MacGregor

A SIGNET BOOK

SIGNET
Published by New American Library, a division of
Penguin Group (USA) Inc., 375 Hudson Street,
New York, New York 10014, USA
Penguin Group (Canada), 90 Eglinton Avenue East, Suite 700, Toronto,
Ontario M4P 2Y3, Canada (a division of Pearson Penguin Canada Inc.)
Penguin Books Ltd., 80 Strand, London WC2R 0RL, England
Penguin Ireland, 25 St. Stephen's Green, Dublin 2,
Ireland (a division of Penguin Books Ltd.)
Penguin Group (Australia), 250 Camberwell Road, Camberwell, Victoria 3124,
Australia (a division of Pearson Australia Group Pty. Ltd.)
Penguin Books India Pvt. Ltd., 11 Community Centre, Panchsheel Park,
New Delhi - 110 017, India
Penguin Group (NZ), 67 Apollo Drive, Rosedale, Auckland 0632,
New Zealand (a division of Pearson New Zealand Ltd.)
Penguin Books (South Africa) (Pty.) Ltd., 24 Sturdee Avenue,
Rosebank, Johannesburg 2196, South Africa

Penguin Books Ltd., Registered Offices:
80 Strand, London WC2R 0RL, England

First Printing, June 2012
10 9 8 7 6 5 4 3 2 1

First published by Signet, an imprint of New American Library,
a division of Penguin Group (USA) Inc.

Copyright © The Estate of Sydney Omarr, 2012
All rights reserved. No part of this book may be reproduced, scanned, or distrib-
uted in any printed or electronic form without permission. Please do not partici-
pate in or encourage piracy of copyrighted materials in violation of the author's
rights. Purchase only authorized editions.

Sydney Omarr's is a registered trademark of Writers House, LLC.

Sydney Omarr® is syndicated worldwide by Los Angeles Times Syndicate.

 REGISTERED TRADEMARK—MARCA REGISTRADA

Printed in the United States of America

PUBLISHER'S NOTE
While the author has made every effort to provide accurate telephone numbers
and Internet addresses at the time of publication, neither the publisher nor the
author assumes any responsibility for errors, or for changes that occur after publication. Further, publisher does not have any control over and does not assume
any responsibility for author or third-party Web sites or their content.

If you purchased this book without a cover you should be aware that this book
is stolen property. It was reported as "unsold and destroyed" to the publisher and
neither the author nor the publisher has received any payment for this "stripped
book."

CONTENTS

CHAPTER 1

Transformation

We branded 2012 the year of the paradigm shift. And since the world didn't end, here we are at the doorstep of 2013, a year of transformation.

The dictionary meaning of the word is straightforward: a change in form, appearance, nature, or character. Astrologically, this kind of change occurs with the slower-moving outer planets—Pluto, Neptune, and Uranus. They exert the greatest influence over our daily lives because they take so long to move through a single sign. Pluto, for instance, entered Capricorn in 2008 and won't leave until early 2024. Neptune, which takes about fourteen years to move through a sign, entered Pisces in early February 2012 and will be there until late January 2026. Uranus entered Aries in March 2011 and leaves that sign in March 2019. So just these three planets extend a powerful influence over a number of years.

The next two planets that influence us over a period of time are Saturn, which takes two and a half years to transit a sign, and Jupiter, which usually takes about a year. Each of these planets is covered extensively in various parts of the book, and each one has its role in the transformation that will prevail in 2013.

In the next chapter we talk about what each of the planets represents, what signs they rule, and just about anything else you could ever want to know about them astrologically. In a later chapter historical perspectives are provided on the three slowest-moving planets. But this chapter, let's take an in-depth look at the planet Uranus and how its energies will help us through this transformation.

Uranus

This planet symbolizes revolution, genius, rebellion, earthquakes, sudden, unexpected events and change, our individuality, inventions and discoveries, electricity, radio, TV, electronics, lightning. You get the idea. Its energy isn't the least bit subtle. It sweeps into our lives, stirs up mass movements, knocks down the old to make way for the new.

It takes eighty-four years for this planet to move through the zodiac. So let's take a trip down memory lane, to the last time Uranus transited the sign of Aries, the warrior. In mid-January 1928 Uranus entered Aries and remained there until late March 1935. Here are some of the events that occurred during this period:

- First air-conditioned office opens in the U.S. in San Antonio
- Scotch tape first marketed by 3M company
- First trans-Atlantic TV image received

- Amelia Earhart first woman to fly the Atlantic—as a passenger
- Alexander Fleming discovers penicillin
- Yo-yo introduced
- First regularly scheduled TV is broadcast three nights a week
- German airship *Graf Zeppelin* begins a round-the-world flight
- Stock market crash
- Salvador Dali's first one-man show
- Bingo invented
- Planet Pluto named
- Hostess Twinkies invented
- N.Y. Yankee Babe Ruth hits three consecutive homers
- First nudist colony open
- First radar detection of planes
- N.Y. *World* reports disappearance of Supreme Court justice Joseph Crater
- N.Y.C college offers first course in radio advertising
- A bloodless coup d'état in Brazil
- First *Dracula* movie released
- Empire State Building opens in N.Y.C.
- Al Capone is indicted on 5,000 counts of prohibition and perjury
- Babe Ruth hits his 600th home run
- Alka Seltzer goes on sale
- Jane Addams first U.S. woman named corecipient of Nobel Peace Prize
- Martial law is declared in Honduras to stop revolt by banana workers fired by United Fruit
- El Salvador army kills 4,000 protesting farmers

3

- First patent issued for a tree, to James Markham for a peach tree
- Amelia Earhart is first woman to fly solo across the Atlantic
- Yellow fever vaccine for humans announced
- U.S. federal gas tax enacted
- Earthquake kills 70,000 in Kansu, China
- Hitler proclaims end of Marxism
- Bank holidays declared in six states to prevent run on banks
- FDR inaugurated as thirty-second president, pledges to pull U.S. out of Depression, and says "We have nothing to fear but fear itself."
- FDR proclaims ten-day bank holiday
- Dachau, first concentration camp, completed
- First flight over Mount Everest
- Nazis stage public book burnings in Germany
- Loch Ness Monster is first reported
- German Secret State Police (Gestapo) established
- In London 500,000 march against anti-Semitism
- Alcatraz officially becomes a federal prison
- *Flash Gordon* comic strip debuts
- FDR signs Home Owners Loan Act
- First Sugar Bowl and first Orange Bowl
- First canned beer is sold
- Monopoly is invented
- First Penguin book is published
- 400,000 demonstrators march against fascism in Madrid
- *Billboard* magazine publishes its first music hit parade
- The first stock car race is held in Daytona Beach, Florida

- *Gone With the Wind* by Margaret Mitchell is published
- Spanish Civil War begins, General Francisco Franco leads uprising
- King Edward VIII abdicates throne to marry Mrs. Wallis Simpson

This list represents just a small sampling of the thousands of events that occurred during Uranus' last transit of Aries. But as you read through this list, you undoubtedly see a pattern, right? War, rebellion, uprisings, numerous discoveries and many "firsts," the rise of Hitler and Nazi Germany, natural disasters such as earthquakes, the completion of engineering marvels like the Empire State Building and Hoover Dam, the precipitous drop of the stock market and the Depression that followed.

Aries is not only the sign of the warrior, but of the entrepreneur, the trailblazer, the one who is so independent and forward thinking that he marches to a different drummer. Aries is fearless, a risk-taker, and like the *Star Trek* motto goes where no man (or woman) has gone before. So when you combine Aries with the planet that symbolizes all the traits mentioned earlier, you have an intriguing MO for transformation and tools for navigating it.

There are two facets for this transformation—planetary and personal. Let's start with the planetary.

Planetary Transformation

If the past holds clues about the kinds of events we might expect during this transit, then let's look at the broad patterns:

Medical breakthroughs. During Uranus' last transit of Aries, the medical breakthroughs were significant: treatment for yellow fever, development of penicillin, anesthesia, insulin shock therapy, vitamin B3, and protonsil, the first sulphur drug, which was used to treat infections caused by streptococcus. So this time around we can expect other types of breakthroughs in medicine, health, pharmacology. A cure for AIDS? Cancer? Heart disease?

Rebellion/revolution. The financial meltdown of 2008, the collapse of the housing market, the shakeout in the job market, the election of the first African-American president: the repercussions of these events are still being felt in early 2013 and are likely to echo for some time. The mix of events has given rise to the Tea Party, racism against Muslims and illegal immigrants, religious intolerance.

The "us versus them" mentality has brought about a wider gap between rich and poor, with the middle class fading rapidly. Groups of urban survivalists have sprung up, some of them extremists. The U.S., with the most powerful military in the world (which also eats up the largest chunk of the federal budget), continues to police the rest of the planet, while pushing the needs of its own citizens into a dark hole labeled *later*.

The contentiousness of the political divide in the U.S. was glaringly obvious in the health-care debate that raged for months. Even though a bill was eventually passed, the right kept on screaming about death panels and the left screamed the bill wasn't comprehensive enough. Meanwhile the cost of health care in the U.S. continues to escalate. These trends, unfortunately, may get worse before Uranus leaves Aries.

However, if we remember that Uranus' job is to shake up the status quo so that new paradigms, new ways of doing things, can be born, then we could see the birth of new political parties that emphasize peace over war. Perhaps we'll see a complete withdrawal of U.S. troops from the Mideast or more demonstrations against war.

New social programs. The meltdown in 2008 resulted in massive bailouts to banks, the collapse of institutions, and billions of stimulus dollars poured into the economy. It was the Obama administration's equivalent of FDR's New Deal, passed during his first term in response to the Great Depression. During this period Social Security was implemented.

As Uranus continues its transit through Aries, we may see the implementation of new social programs—such as universal health care mentioned above—or new economic programs that aid people rather than banks and corporations.

Discoveries. Numerous discoveries and inventions came about during Uranus' last pass through Aries. This transit could produce the twenty-first-century equivalents in technology, television, the Internet, health and medicine, engineering, movies, earthquake detection, music, ebooks, alternative fuels.

World records. During Uranus' last transit of Aries many "firsts" occurred, and world records were set.

This time around we could see more of the same—in space flight, cars that run on alternative fuels, high-speed trains, athletics, even the ways our homes and office buildings are powered. The world may go green more quickly than we can imagine.

With Uranus we either embrace change—or it's forced upon us. So let's take a look at how each of us can embrace the change Uranus promises to usher in.

Aries ♈

Cardinal fire sign

As the go-getter of the zodiac, you're probably enjoying Uranus' transit through your sign. It brings all the excitement and adrenaline-powered events that make you feel *alive*.

That said, you generally aren't fond of sudden, unexpected change unless you initiate it. If no area of your life has gone stale or become an empty ritual, then Uranus won't be thrusting anything on you, Aries. You can simply enjoy the wild ride. But if your job, relationships, or career are on remote control, then this transit could be quite a shock, with an abundance of unexpected upsets and changes. Where do you fall in the scheme of things? Uranus has been in Aries for about two years now, so you should have a fairly clear idea how the transit is affecting you.

The best way for you to navigate this transit is to do what you do naturally: maintain a sense of adventure about life; be passionate in all that you undertake; keep your steady focus, don't hesitate to explore. In addition, treat others the way you like to be treated.

In love relationships, strive to be more cooperative, to see things the way your partner does. In your career, with your creative work, complete what you start.

Unusual ideas and idiosyncratic individuals are part of this transit package. You won't be bored, but be careful that life doesn't become just one adrenaline high after the other. Welcome change, embrace it, even if it's thrust on you.

Taurus ♉
Fixed earth sign

You're the most stubborn, resilient, and resolute sign in the zodiac. It's why Taurus is symbolized by the bull! As a fixed earth sign, you like things in your life to be orderly, practical, even predictable. You're slow to change your opinions and beliefs. Stability is your middle name.

The Uranus transit is occurring in your solar twelfth house—your personal unconscious, the most hidden part of your chart. It means that Uranus shakes up your world from the inside out. Issues you have buried, power you have disowned, dreams you've forgotten—all of it surfaces during this transit. Your greatest strength during this period is to tackle one issue at a time and deal with it the way you do everything else in your life—carefully, thoroughly, meticulously. Your dreams should be especially vivid during this transit, and it's to your advantage to remember them, work with them. They contain insights and information that are important.

Unusual people should enter your life during this

transit. Some are teachers, others are students; all will play vital roles. They may disappear as suddenly and inexplicably as they appear.

Gemini ♊

Mutable air sign

Your greatest strengths are your flexibility and communication ability. Both qualities will be enhanced during the Uranus transit through Aries, which forms a beneficial angle to your sun. This transit may not be all bells and whistles; it's a bit more subtle than that. But it brings excitement, change, and unusual people and experiences.

It occurs in your solar eleventh house of friends, wishes, and dreams. More group participation is likely—in theater, writing, bridge, esoterica. Whatever your interests and passions, you find a group of like-minded individuals who share them. In some way they help you to achieve your wishes and dreams.

New opportunities should surface for self-expression. If you've always had a secret yearning to write a novel or screenplay, for example, then this transit helps you to do it. If you're an amateur photographer, you may have an opportunity to become a professional. The transit will free you from limiting circumstances—a relationship that no longer works, a job that has grown stale and predictable, a career that no longer feels right. Your comfortable ruts will become history.

Cancer ♋
Cardinal water sign

The lens through which you see the world is personal, subjective, emotional. Your nurturing and intuitive abilities are your greatest strengths and will serve you well during this transit. Let's take a closer look.

This transit falls in your solar tenth house—career, public persona—and forms a challenging angle to your sun. Abrupt, unexpected changes may challenge your chosen professional course. Your job, for example, could be outsourced. Or you get a new boss whom you don't like. Or you have to take a cut in pay. Whatever the curve ball that Uranus in Aries throws your way, Cancer, you should strive to see it as an opportunity. When the transit is over, you will look back and realize it was exactly that.

When the rug is pulled out from under you, you're forced to use your greatest strengths to forge a new path, a new way of being. So don't hesitate to draw on your intuition during this transit. Seek out the new, the different. Embrace change.

Leo ♌

Fixed fire sign

The transit of Uranus through Aries should be right up your alley, Leo. It forms a beneficial angle with your sun and bolsters all the qualities for which you're known and loved—warmth, compassion, flair for drama, ability to make friends with just about anyone.

This transit should bring about sudden, exciting change in your life. New opportunities for creative self-expression surface, and you find yourself feeling more free and buoyant than you have in years. You meet stimulating people, individuals who may be geniuses in their fields and who prove helpful to you in some way. There could be romance and love with this transit too, Leo. So many intriguing individuals are entering your life now that you'll have your pick!

You may travel abroad unexpectedly, for business, pleasure, or both. You might go to college, grad school, law school. You're looking for new knowledge and insights and could study astrology, the I Ching, tarot, or other divination systems. This is a great period to set up a regular exercise regimen if you don't have one already. You also should consider yoga.

Virgo ♍

Mutable earth sign

You're the perfectionist of the zodiac, detail oriented and precise in just about everything you do. These qualities prove helpful during the Uranus transit through Aries, which occurs in your solar eighth house. Let's take a closer, more detailed look.

Sudden, unexpected events and experiences may force you to break away from limitations and restrictions that make you feel trapped. These limitations and restrictions were either self-imposed or imposed on you by others. Whatever the source, you now make decisions to break free of these limitations. You feel as if the restrictions are eating away at your soul. If a job has made you feel this way, then you take definite steps to get out of the situation. If a relationship is the source of your feelings, then you end it. One way or another, restrictions become intolerable, and you bust free.

Since the eighth house represents joint resources, your partner's income may rise or fall suddenly, unexpectedly. You could inherit money. It's an excellent time to get out of debt. In fact, debt may be another limitation that you find intolerable.

Any new romance that comes your way could be highly sexual and have a deeply intuitive component to it.

Libra ♎

Cardinal air sign

One of your greatest strengths is your ability to interact with people. It's not just a social thing for you, either. You generally enjoy people and exploring what makes them tick. This ability will serve you well through the Uranus transit in Aries.

Uranus is now moving in opposition to your sun, through your solar seventh house, so your closest partnerships—romantic and business—are impacted. Sudden, unexpected events bring about the beginning and end of partnerships and force you to stand up for who you are and what you really believe. In doing so, you break free of restrictions that have become unbearable.

This transit may seem harsh at times. It appears that stuff is happening *to* you, that the universe is ganging up against you. But what's actually happening is that energies you have repressed over the years are now scrambling for release. Any relationship that ends under this transit—through death or otherwise—does so because it has served its purpose. Relationships that begin during this transit are apt to be exciting, different in some way, and stimulating mentally, emotionally, and spiritually.

To navigate this transit successfully, it's best not to resist events. Just go with the flow. Your creative self-expression during this period is important. Express what you feel when you feel it. If you hold your emotions inside, it could result in health problems or accidents. One way or another, the emotions find expression. Keep in mind that the whole purpose of this transit is to free you.

Scorpio ♏

Fixed water sign

Your greatest strengths are your uncanny intuition and ability to delve deeply for answers. During the Uranus transit through Aries, these qualities are heightened.

This transit is about freedom—from restrictions and limitations in any area of your life that prevent you from evolving creatively, spiritually, emotionally. As a fixed water sign, you probably don't like change any more than your fixed-sign brothers—Taurus, Leo, and Aquarius. But change you must. It's easier if you can learn to embrace change rather than resist it so that it isn't thrust on you.

Since this transit occurs in your solar sixth house, the

area most likely to be impacted is your daily work routine and health. The possible scenarios depend on how rigid, routine, or boring your daily work is; whether you stick to this work primarily because it's comfortable; and whether or not you enjoy what you're doing. The health aspect depends on how well you take care of yourself and your beliefs about health. In other words, if you believe that people get colds every winter, then you probably will get a cold every winter. So take inventory of your beliefs, Scorpio!

Sagittarius ♐
Mutable fire sign

The Uranus transit through fellow fire sign Aries is an adventure for you, exciting and stimulating, with the kind of surprises you enjoy. It occurs in your solar fifth house of love and romance, creativity, and children. It's likely that romantic relationships begin and end suddenly, that your creativity is taking you in new directions, and that everything you enjoy takes on a brighter patina.

With Uranus in Aries forming a beneficial angle to your sun, you're able to become who you really are. Your creative self-expression shines forth, and new venues for creativity open up. You may find yourself involved in projects that are totally different from anything you've done before that prompt you to stretch your creativity in new ways.

In romance and love relationships that no longer serve your best interests will end, and new relationships that are more in line with your needs and desires will begin. Your sexuality is heightened, and sex may be a large component of any relationship that begins during this seven-year transit.

If you're a Sadge who enjoys travel—and you probably are, many of your sign do—then you'll be doing more of it during this transit. You might move too, if you find a place that is more in line with the new you.

Capricorn ♑
Cardinal earth sign

You're known for your focus, clarity about your goals, and ability to plow through any obstacle you encounter. All of these traits will serve you well during the Uranus transit through Aries. However, since this transit forms a challenging angle to your sun sign, you may have to make some adjustments in your approach, Capricorn.

During this transit any limitations or restrictions that are self-imposed or imposed on you by others will become unbearable. Sudden, unexpected events will create situations that enable you to break free of these restrictions, but the events seem to come out of nowhere and may be upsetting. The transit occurs in your solar fourth house—your domestic environment—so let's take a look at some possible scenarios:

Your parents move in with you.

Your employer is relocating, and if you want to keep your job, you have to move too.

Your partner or spouse is laid off work, and you have to sell your home and move to a smaller place.

Your parents get divorced, and you have to relocate.

You get the idea here. The fourth house represents the foundation of your life, the most intimate and personal part of who you are. For most of us, changes in this area can be deeply unsettling. Any part of this area that has grown stale, rigid, or routine will be affected. But if your home life is vibrant and exciting, then it won't be impacted. Just try to be as flexible as you can; embrace the changes that come your way. This transit is intended to free you emotionally, creatively, and spiritually.

Aquarius ♒

Fixed air sign

The Uranus transit through Aries forms a beneficial angle to your sun, so you've got plenty to look forward to, Aquarius. This transit occurs in your solar third house, which represents communication, your conscious mind, neighborhood and neighbors, siblings, daily life, travel. This area is where you're apt to experience all the excitement of this transit. Let's take a closer look.

At this time your consciousness is expanding, leaping outward, seeking new ideas, exploring different belief systems and lifestyles. You may move quite suddenly and unexpectedly, but it turns out to be beneficial for you. You may undertake creative projects that are outside your usual talents and abilities and discover a new facet of your personality. This period is all about trying the new and unexplored, about adventures in consciousness and communication.

It's the ideal time to start a blog, build a Web site,

or write a novel or other book. Get involved in community activities. Get out and meet new people. Network. Enjoy yourself. Uranus, the planet that rules your sign, won't disappoint you during this transit. To enhance the effects of this transit, strive to be flexible, to go with the flow.

Pisces ✕

Mutable water sign

Like your mutable siblings—Gemini, Virgo, and Sagittarius—you don't have any problem with change. But because this transit occurs in a fire sign, Aries, your solar second house of finances, it's a good idea to take an honest look at your finances.

How do you earn your living? Is it in line with your beliefs and ideals? Has it grown stale, are you just going through the motions? If so, then Uranus in Aries may shake up your financial picture to the point where you must take steps to rectify things. You may take a second job, for instance, thinking the additional income will help, but then that job turns into the job of your dreams. Or you could get laid off, and it turns out to be the best thing that ever happened to you, just the nudge you need to launch your own business.

Your imagination and intuition prove helpful during this transit. Be sure to listen to your intuition and allow your imagination to take you places you've never been before. Nothing is too wild to try, too *out there* to consider. However, here are some suggestions for making this transit a bit easier: pay cash for everything, get rid of your credit card debt, stick to a budget.

CHAPTER 2

Astro Basics

On the day you were born, what was the weather like? If you were born at night, had the moon already risen? Was it full or the shape of a Cheshire cat's grin? Was the delivery ward quiet or bustling with activity? Unless your mom or dad has a very good memory, you'll probably never know the full details. But there's one thing you can know for sure: on the day you were born the sun was located in a particular zone of the zodiac, an imaginary 360-degree belt that circles the Earth. The belt is divided into twelve 30-degree portions called signs.

If you were born between July 23 and August 22, then the sun was passing through the sign of Leo, so we say that your sun sign is Leo. Each of the twelve signs has distinct attributes and characteristics. Leos, for instance, love being the center of attention. They're warm, compassionate people with a flair for the dramatic. Virgos, born between August 23 and September 22, are perfectionists with discriminating intellects and a genius for details. Capricorns, born between December 22 and January 19, are the worker bees of the zodiac, serious minded, ambitious, industrious.

How Signs Are Classified

As you probably gathered from the first chapter, the twelve signs are categorized according to element and quality or modality. The first category, element, reads like a basic science lesson—fire, earth, air, and water—and describes the general physical characteristics of the signs.

Fire signs—Aries, Leo, Sagittarius—are warm, dynamic individuals who are always passionate about what they do.

Earth signs—Taurus, Virgo, Capricorn—are the builders of the zodiac, practical and efficient, grounded in everything they do.

Air signs—Gemini, Libra, Aquarius—are people who live mostly in the world of ideas. They are terrific communicators.

Water signs—Cancer, Scorpio, Pisces—live through their emotions, imaginations, and intuitions.

The second category describes how each sign operates in the physical world, how adaptable it is to circumstances.

Cardinal signs—Aries, Cancer, Libra, Capricorn—are initiators. These people are active, impatient, restless. They're great at starting things, but unless a project or relationship holds their attention, they lose interest and may not finish what they start.

Fixed signs—Taurus, Leo, Scorpio, Aquarius—are deliberate, controlled, resolute. These individuals tend to move more slowly than cardinal signs, are often stubborn, and resist change. They seek roots and stability and are always in the game for the long haul. They aren't quitters.

Mutable signs—Gemini, Virgo, Sagittarius, Pisces—are adaptable. These people are flexible, changeable, communicative. They don't get locked into rigid patterns or belief systems.

SUN SIGNS

Sign	Date	Element	Quality
Aries ♈	March 21–April 19	Fire	Cardinal
Taurus ♉	April 20–May 20	Earth	Fixed
Gemini ♊	May 21–June 21	Air	Mutable
Cancer ♋	June 22–July 22	Water	Cardinal
Leo ♌	July 23–August 22	Fire	Fixed
Virgo ♍	August 23–September 22	Earth	Mutable
Libra ♎	September 23–October 22	Air	Cardinal
Scorpio ♏	October 23–November 21	Water	Fixed
Sagittarius ♐	November 22–December 21	Fire	Mutable
Capricorn ♑	December 22–January 19	Earth	Cardinal
Aquarius ♒	January 20–February 18	Air	Fixed
Pisces ♓	February 19–March 20	Water	Mutable

The Planets

The planets in astrology are the players who make things happen. They're the characters in the story of your life. This story always begins with the sun, the giver of life.

Your sun sign describes your self-expression, your primal energy, the essence of who you are. It's the archetypal pattern of your Self. When you know another person's sun sign, you already have a great deal of information about that person. Let's say you're a Taurus who has just started dating a Gemini. How compatible are you?

On the surface, it wouldn't seem that you have much in common. Taurus is a fixed earth sign; Gemini is a mutable air sign. Taurus is persistent, stubborn, practical, a cultivator as opposed to an initiator. Gemini is a chameleon, a communicator, social, with a mind as quick as lightning. Taurus is ruled by Venus, which governs the arts, money, beauty, love, and romance. Gemini is ruled by Mercury, which governs communication and travel. There doesn't seem to be much common ground. But before we write off this combination, let's look a little deeper.

Suppose the Taurus has Mercury in Gemini, and the Gemini has Venus in Taurus? This would mean that the Taurus and Gemini each have their rulers in the other person's sign. They probably communicate well and enjoy travel and books (Mercury) and would see eye to eye on romance, art, and music (Venus). They might get along so well, in fact, that they collaborate on creative projects.

Each of us is also influenced by the other nine planets (the sun and moon are treated like planets in astrology) and the signs they were transiting when we were born. Suppose our Taurus and Gemini have the same moon sign? The moon rules our inner needs, emotions and intuition, and all that makes us feel secure within ourselves. Quite often compatible moon signs can overcome even the most glaring difference in sun signs because the two people share similar emotions.

In the section on predictions your sun sign always

takes center stage, and every prediction is based on the movement of the transiting planets in relation to your sun sign. Let's say you're a Sagittarius. Between October 7 and November 5 this year Venus will be transiting your sign. What does this mean for you? Well, since Venus rules—among other things—romance, you can expect your love life to pick up significantly during these weeks. Other people will find you attractive and be more open to your ideas, and you'll radiate a certain charisma. Your creative endeavors will move full steam ahead.

The planets table provides an overview of the planets and the signs that they rule. Keep in mind that the moon is the swiftest-moving planet, changing signs about every two and a half days, and that Pluto is the snail of the zodiac, taking as long as thirty years to transit a single sign. Although the faster-moving planets—the moon, Mercury, Venus, and Mars—have an impact on our lives, it's the slow pokes—Uranus, Neptune, and Pluto—that bring about the most profound influence and change. Jupiter and Saturn fall between the others in terms of speed. This year Jupiter spends the first six months in Gemini, then enters Cancer on June 25 and doesn't leave that sign until July 16, 2014.

In the section on predictions the most frequent references are to the transits of Mercury, Venus, and Mars and the movements of the transiting moon.

Now glance through the planets table. When a sign is in parentheses, it means the planet corules that sign. This assignation dates back to when we thought there were only seven planets in the solar system. But since there were still twelve signs, some of the planets had to do double duty!

THE PLANETS

Planet	Rules	Attributes of Planet
Sun ☉	Leo	self-expression, primal energy, creative ability, ego, individuality
Moon ☽	Cancer	emotions, intuition, mother or wife, security
Mercury ☿	Gemini, Virgo	intellect, mental acuity, communication, logic, reasoning, travel, contracts
Venus ♀	Taurus, Libra	love, romance, beauty, artistic instincts, the arts, music, material and financial resources
Mars ♂	Aries (Scorpio)	physical and sexual energy, aggression, drive
Jupiter ♃	Sagittarius (Pisces)	luck, expansion, success, prosperity, growth, creativity, spiritual interests, higher education, law
Saturn ♄	Capricorn (Aquarius)	laws of physical universe, discipline, responsibility, structure, karma, authority
Uranus ♅	Aquarius	individuality, genius, eccentricity, originality, science, revolution
Neptune ♆	Pisces	visionary self, illusions, what's hidden, psychic ability, dissolution of ego boundaries, spiritual insights, dreams

Planet	Rules	Attributes of Planet
Pluto ♀ ♇	Scorpio	the darker side, death, sex, regeneration, rebirth, profound and permanent change, transformation

Houses and Rising Signs

In the instant you drew your first breath, one of the signs of the zodiac was just passing over the eastern horizon. Astrologers refer to this as the rising sign or ascendant. It's what makes your horoscope unique. Think of your ascendant as the front door of your horoscope, the place where you enter into this life and begin your journey.

Your ascendant is based on the exact moment of your birth, and the other signs follow counterclockwise. If you have Taurus rising, for example, that is the cusp of your first house. The cusp of the second would be Gemini, of the third Cancer, and so on around the horoscope circle in a counterclockwise direction. Each house governs a particular area of life, which is outlined below.

The best way to find out your rising sign is to have your horoscope drawn up by an astrologer. For those of you with access to the Internet, though, there are several sites that provide free birth horoscopes: www.astro.com and www.cafeastrology.com are two good ones.

In a horoscope the ascendant (cusp of the first house), IC (cusp of the fourth house), descendant (cusp of the seventh house), and MC (cusp of the tenth house) are considered to be the most critical angles. Any planets that fall close to these angles are extremely important in the overall astrological picture of who you are. By the same token, planets that fall in the first, fourth, seventh, and tenth houses are also considered to be important.

Now here's a rundown on what the houses mean.

Ascendant or Rising: The First of Four Important Critical Angles in a Horoscope

- How other people see you
- How you present yourself to the world
- Your physical appearance

First House, Personality

- Early childhood
- Your ego
- Your body type and how you feel about your body
- General physical health
- Defense mechanisms
- Your creative thrust

Second House, Personal Values

- How you earn and spend your money
- Your personal values
- Your material resources and assets
- Your attitudes and beliefs toward money
- Your possessions and your attitude toward those possessions
- Your self-worth
- Your attitudes about creativity

Third House, Communication and Learning

- Personal expression
- Intellect and mental attitudes and perceptions
- Siblings, neighbors, and relatives
- How you learn
- School until college
- Reading, writing, teaching
- Short trips (the grocery store versus Europe in seven days)
- Earth-bound transportation
- Creativity as a communication device

IC or Fourth House Cusp: The Second Critical Angle in a Horoscope

- Sign on IC describes the qualities and traits of your home during early childhood
- Describes roots of your creative abilities and talents

Fourth House, Your Roots

- Personal/domestic environment
- Your home
- Your attitudes toward family
- Early childhood conditioning
- Real estate
- Your nurturing parent

Some astrologers say this house belongs to Mom or her equivalent in your life, others say it belongs to

Dad or his equivalent. It makes sense to us that it's Mom because the fourth house is ruled by the moon, which rules mothers. But in this day and age, when parental roles are in flux, the only hard and fast rule is that the fourth belongs to the parent who nurtures you most of the time.

- The conditions at the end of your life
- Early childhood support of your creativity and interests

Fifth House, Children and Creativity

- Kids, your first-born in particular
- Love affairs, romance
- What you enjoy
- Creative ability
- Gambling and speculation
- Pets

Traditionally, pets belong in the sixth house. But that definition stems from the days when "pets" were chattel. These days we don't even refer to them as pets. They are animal companions who bring us pleasure.

Sixth House, Work and Responsibility

- Day-to-day working conditions and environment
- Competence and skills
- Your experience of employees and employers
- Duty to work, to employees
- Health and the daily maintenance of your health

Descendant/Seventh House Cusp: The Third Critical Angle in a Horoscope

- The sign on the house cusp describes the qualities sought in intimate or business relationships
- Describes qualities of creative partnerships

Seventh House, Partnerships and Marriage

- Marriage
- Marriage partner
- Significant others
- Business partnerships
- Close friends
- Open enemies
- Contracts

Eighth House: Transformation

- Sexuality as transformation
- Secrets
- Death, taxes, inheritances, insurance, mortgages, and loans
- Resources shared with others
- Your partner's finances
- The occult (read: astrology, reincarnation, UFOs, everything weird and strange)
- Your hidden talents
- Psychology
- Life-threatening illnesses
- Your creative depths

Ninth House, Worldview

- Philosophy and religion
- The law, courts, judicial system
- Publishing
- Foreign travels and cultures
- College, graduate school
- Spiritual beliefs
- Travel abroad

MC or Cusp of Tenth House: The Fourth Critical Angle in a Horoscope

- Sign on cusp of MC describes qualities you seek in a profession
- Your public image
- Your creative and professional achievements

Tenth House, Profession and Career

- Public image as opposed to a job that merely pays the bills (sixth house)
- Your status and position in the world
- The authoritarian parent and authority in general
- People who hold power over you
- Your public life
- Your career/profession

Eleventh House, Ideals and Dreams

- Peer groups
- Social circles (your writers' group, your mother's bridge club)

- Your dreams and aspirations
- How you can realize your dreams

Twelfth House, Personal Unconscious

- Power you have disowned that must be claimed again
- Institutions — hospitals, prisons, nursing homes — and what is hidden
- What you must confront this time around, your karma, issues brought in from other lives
- Psychic gifts and abilities
- Healing talents
- What you give unconditionally

In the section on predictions you'll find references to transiting planets moving into certain houses. These houses are actually solar houses that are created by putting your sun sign on the ascendant. This technique is how most predictions are made for the general public rather than for specific individuals.

Lunations

Every year there are twelve new moons and twelve full moons, with some years having thirteen full moons. The extra full moon is called the Blue Moon. New moons are typically when we should begin new projects, set new goals, seek new opportunities. They're times for beginnings. They usher in new opportunities according to house and sign.

Two weeks after each new moon, there's a full moon.

This is the time of harvest, fruition, when we reap what we've sown.

Whenever a new moon falls in your sign, take time to brainstorm what you would like to achieve during weeks and months until the full moon falls in your sign. These goals can be in any area of your life. Or you can simply take the time on each new moon to set up goals and strategies for what you would like to achieve or manifest during the next two weeks—until the full moon—or until the next new moon.

Here's a list of all the new moons and full moons during 2013. The asterisk beside any new-moon entry indicates a solar eclipse; the asterisk next to a full-moon entry indicates a lunar eclipse.

LUNATIONS OF 2013

New Moons

January 11—Capricorn
February 10—Aquarius
March 11—Pisces
April 10—Aries
*May 9—Taurus
June 8—Gemini
July 8—Cancer
August 6—Leo
September 5—Virgo
October 4—Libra
*November 3—Scorpio
December 2—Sagittarius

Full Moons

January 26—Leo
February 25—Virgo
March 27—Libra
*April 25—Scorpio
*May 25—Sagittarius
June 23—Capricorn
July 22—Aquarius
August 20—Aquarius
September 19—Pisces
*October 18—Aries
November 17—Taurus
December 17—Gemini

Every year there are two lunar and two solar eclipses, separated from each other by about two weeks. Lunar eclipses tend to deal with emotional issues and our internal world and often bring an emotional issue to the surface related to the sign and house in which the eclipse falls. They can also result in news. Solar eclipses deal with events and often enable us to see something that has eluded us. They also symbolize beginnings and endings.

Read more about eclipses in the Big Picture for your sign for 2013. I also recommend Celeste Teal's excellent book, *Eclipses*.

Mercury Retrograde

Every year Mercury—the planet that symbolizes communication and travel—turns retrograde three times. During these periods our travel plans often go awry, communication breaks down, computers go berserk, cars or appliances develop problems. You get the idea. Things in our daily lives don't work as smoothly as we would like.

Here are some guidelines to follow for Mercury retrogrades:

Try not to travel. But if you have to, be flexible and think of it as an adventure. If you're stuck overnight in an airport in Houston or Atlanta, though, the adventure part of this could be a stretch.

Don't sign contracts—unless you don't mind revisiting them when Mercury is direct again.

Communicate as succinctly and clearly as possible.

Back up all computer files. Use an external hard drive and/or a flash drive. If you've had a computer crash, you already know how frustrating it can be to reconstruct your files.

Don't buy expensive electronics. Expensive anything.

Don't submit manuscripts, screenplays, pitch ideas, or launch new projects.

Revise, rewrite, rethink, review.

In the overview for each sign, check out the dates for this year's Mercury retrogrades and how these retrogrades are likely to impact you. Do the same for eclipses.

Other Retrogrades

Every planet except the sun and moon turns retrograde. So let's look at the retrogrades that will occur in 2013.

Venus: December 21, 2013, to January 31, 2014. When Venus is retrograde, your personal relationships often suffer from miscommunication, your love life is bumpy, romance can be withheld or minimized.

Mars: No retrogrades this year for Mars!

Jupiter: January 30 to November 7. Ouch. It's troublesome to have the planet of luck and expansion retrograde for so long. During this period your finances may be depressed, your luck factor isn't operating at full potential, and there could be setbacks or delays with publishing and educational ventures.

Saturn: February 18 to July 7. During this retrograde you discover which structures in your life need bolstering. Profits may be depressed.

Uranus: July 17 to December 17. Upheavals and changes occur within your inner life. You may not be quite as sharp and on top of things.

Neptune: June 6 to November 13. Your creativity and your ability to envision what you desire are limited in some way.

Pluto: April 12 to September 20. You may feel powerless or unmotivated in some area of your life.

△ CHAPTER 3

Romance, Love, and Creativity in 2013

Even during a year of transformation we still fall in love and get married, our creative muses are still whispering in our ears, our lives march on. For some of us our greatest transformation this year will unfold through romance, love, and creative ventures. So let's take a closer look at how each sun sign approaches love and romance and what types of creative activities they might be able to turn into gold.

Aries

Your passions are legendary. You're impulsive when it comes to matters of the heart and tend to leap in with both feet and ask questions later. Once you're involved you're involved completely and totally and want your partner to declare his or her undying love for you. The problem with this approach occurs when your partner doesn't feel the same way you do. Then jealousy and possessiveness creep in, Aries, and things can get muddled quickly.

Your freedom and independence are paramount to

your happiness, so you need a partner who understands and respects your space. But because you're a stranger to compromise, a vital part of any relationship, you may find intimate relationships challenging. Once you're involved, your passions are fierce and can easily topple into the dark extremes of jealousy, possessiveness, suspicion.

Your entrepreneurial and fearless spirit enjoys a partner who can compete with you on any level—on those long hikes into the wilderness, in the boardroom, in the classroom, in the garage out back where you're building your newest invention. You get the idea here, right, Aries? Boredom is your nemesis. So which signs are good matches for you? Let's take a closer look at some of the possibilities.

Sagittarius. This fellow fire sign will give you all the freedom you crave—and then some. She'll match you joke for joke, drink for drink. If she's the physical type, and many of them are, she'll match you on those hikes. But for a Sadge those hikes may be in some far-flung spot like Tibet. Like you, Sadge pushes herself, but she's more adaptable than you are. Sometimes she may come off like a know-it-all. But overall this combination holds great promise.

Gemini. This air sign's wit, versatility, and ability to talk about virtually anything appeal to you. He's generally not possessive, either, a major plus when you're in one of your darker moods. His mind is sharp and lightning quick, and he probably has a vast, complicated network of friends and acquaintances. Also appealing. So what're the negatives? Gemini generally isn't as independent as you are and may spend more time with his friends than he does with you. But overall this combination is lively, fun, and never boring.

Leo. Another fire sign. On the surface it looks like a good match. Leo possesses an infinite capacity for enjoyment, which appeals to you. But she also loves having center stage—not just sometimes, but most of the time—and that can be a major turnoff for you.

Libra, Aquarius. Libra is your opposite sign. The match could be fantastic because you balance each other. Where you're the loner, she's the social butterfly. You're independent, she's a networker with more friends than a hive has bees. Whether this works or not depends on the signs of your natal moons, ascendants, and Venus. You and Aquarius could be a winning combination. His independence matches yours, he's as sharp as the proverbial tack, and he pulls no punches in expressing what he wants, when he wants it. Downside? He may not be as physical or competitive and lives much of his life in his head.

What about another *Aries*? Depends on the signs of your moons. Strictly on the basis of sun signs, you're both so independent the relationship may never get off the ground!

Creatively, your interests span the spectrum of possibilities. So take your greatest passion and then study the market to find out how you might fill any gap that you identify. You excel at going where no one else dares to venture, Aries.

Taurus

As a sensual earth sign you love beautiful surroundings, good food, art, music, books. You tend to keep things to yourself, so a lot goes on beneath the surface that others don't see. You usually don't leap into a relationship, like Aries, but test the waters, discovering the other person's interests, passions, seeking commonalities in worldviews. Once you do get involved you're a considerate, loving, and sensual partner who expects the same level of commitment in return.

You're a stable individual, grounded and practical, but many of you have a deeper interest in the unknown, the unseen, the mysterious. If you find a partner who shares that interest in esoteric ideas, then you can overlook things in the relationship that may not work exactly as you would like. Communication, Taurus, is key for you.

You aren't into drama, artifice, flamboyance—not for yourself and not in a partner either. But you enjoy a partner who is physically attractive or who has a particular artistic gift that you appreciate—music, art, a way with words, anything that appeals to your senses.

If you're a Taurus who is into sports and health, and many of them are, then a health-conscious partner is a major plus. But there's another side to you too, an inner mystic, a quiet, observant Buddha who remains calm and centered, in tune with unseen forces. You would do well with a partner who possesses those qualities as well.

Leo, Sagittarius, Aries. Unless you have a moon, rising, or Venus in one of those signs, the fire signs probably won't work for you. Too much drama, boisterous behavior, and anger to suit your tastes.

Virgo, Capricorn. Fellow earth signs. Virgo could be the ticket. She's as practical as you are and, in many instances, just as mystical. Capricorn is focused and as physical as you are, but may not be as mystically inclined.

Scorpio. Your opposite sign, so there may be a good balance. She's secretive and can be vengeful, but she's just as mystical as you are.

On the creative front you're in for the long haul. You aren't a quitter. Once you uncover your passion, you go for it big time and never give up.

Gemini

For you seduction begins with the mind, with ideas. Any prospective partner that fails to interest you intellectually doesn't remain long on your radar. You're the consummate communicator of the zodiac, the networker, so any relationship in which you're involved must have that communication component. Otherwise it probably won't last.

You're up front about what you feel, but those feelings could change at a moment's notice, a dichotomy that can be confusing to a partner. And to everyone else around you, for that matter. No wonder your sign is represented by the twins.

For you everything starts with a single burning question: *why?* You then set about finding out why and in the course of your journey may be distracted by a million other pieces of information that are eventually integrated into your quest. This means, of course, that your journey toward the why of the original question may not end in *this* lifetime! So you need a partner whose curiosity matches your own.

Sagittarius, Aries. Sadge is your opposite sign. He matches you in curiosity, but may not be up to snuff in other areas. With Aries there's never a dull moment. She's a match for your quickness and wit, but may not have the curiosity you do about other people.

Libra and Aquarius. Usually compatible in that both signs value information and communication.

Water signs. Oddly, Pisces might be a good match because it's the only other sign represented by two of something. And his imagination will appeal to you.

Creatively, you excel at anything that involves communication. Better dust off that novel, Gemini, and start rewriting!

Cancer

In romance it's always about feelings first—not the mind, not even the body, but *emotions.* Your partner has to be as dedicated to her inner world as you are to yours, so that your inner worlds can, well, *merge.* That's the ideal. Yet because you're a cardinal sign, like Aries, Libra, and Capricorn, there's a certain independence in you that demands emotional space. Contradictory, but not to you.

Despite your emotional depth, you tend to avoid confrontations. Like the crab that symbolizes your sign you retreat into your shell at the first sign of trouble. Yet how can you smooth out anything in a relationship if you can't discuss disagreements? It's as if you expect disagreements to be ironed out telepathically. If that's true, then your best matches romantically are probably other water signs. Let's take a deeper look.

Pisces, Scorpio. Both signs are as psychic as you are but in different ways. Pisces is the softer of the two signs, dreamier. Scorpio might overwhelm you but gives you the emotional space you need.

Taurus. A good match. This earth sign helps you to ground yourself in the real world and gives you emotional space—maybe more than you need!

Capricorn, Virgo. Cappy is your opposite sign, so the possibility of balance is there. Virgo might be too picky for your tastes but shows you how to communicate verbally.

Air signs? Fire signs? Not so good, unless you have a moon, ascendant, Venus, or Mars in one of those signs.

Creatively, you excel at anything in which you can use your intuition and emotional power.

Leo

You've got enough passion for all the other signs in the zodiac—and then some. That passion is often linked to the attention of others, which probably explains why so many actors and actresses have a Leo sun, moon, or ascendant. Your life is about drama, and the higher the drama the deeper your passion. It's that passion that busts through obstacles, that burns a path toward where you want to go in both life and love.

Your compassion extends to anyone in a tough situation—or to any creature that needs love and reassurance that we humans aren't heartless. So let's be real here. Your partner, whoever he or she is, probably has to love animals the way you do. Even if there are twenty strays in your backyard, your partner must be amenable to the idea that you feed the multitudes. Not an easy request, says the universe. But there are some strong possibilities.

Sagittarius, Aries. Fellow fire signs. Sadge, symbolized by a creature that is half human and half horse, usually has animal companions—not pets, but *companions.* There's a big difference. She's your match in the compassion area. She understands your need to connect to an audience, but she may not stick around to be a part of that audience. The energy match with Aries is great. But unless you've got a moon, ascendant, or Venus in Aries, she may not shower you—or your animal companions—with enough attention.

Gemini, Libra. These two air signs could be excellent matches for you, Leo. You'll enjoy Gemini's lively intellect and Libra's artistic sensibilities.

Creatively, you excel at anything connected to drama, fashion, politics.

Virgo

You're the absolute master of details. You collect massive amounts of information, sift through it all with an eye for what works and what doesn't, and toss out everything that is extraneous. Your quest for perfection is never compromised. It's evident in the inner work you do, honing your own psyche, and in everything you take on in the external world. These qualities can make a romantic partnership somewhat challenging because your partner goes under the same microscope that everything else does.

You're a layered individual and benefit from a partner who understands that and knows how to peel away those layers without making you feel vulnerable or exposed. A partner who enjoys every single one of those layers. So who's your best match?

Taurus and Capricorn. Fellow earth signs. Taurus takes all the time the relationship needs to peel away the layers of your personality so she could find the gold at your core. She's patient, resolute, determined. Capricorn might consider the relationship as just one more challenge to be conquered but could provide a nice balance to your penchant for details.

Cancer, Scorpio. These two water signs complement you. Cancer grasps who you are emotionally but may not be as willing as you are to discuss elements of the relationship. Since your sign is ruled by Mercury, the planet of communication, that could be a drawback. Scorpio's emotional intensity could be overwhelming but he'll be delighted to peel away the layers of your personality!

Gemini. Even though air and earth aren't usually compatible, Gemini and Virgo share Mercury as a ruler. Communication in this combination is likely to be strong and fluid, with a constant exchange of ideas.

On the creative front, your specialty is details: editor, writer, mystic, researcher, anything involving health and medicine.

Libra

There's a certain duality in your psychological makeup that isn't mentioned very often. It's not due to a penchant for secrecy or deviousness but to a reluctance to hurt anyone's feelings. As a result you often find yourself paralyzed by indecision. *Who do I really love? A or B?* Since you don't want to hurt either person, you maintain both relationships and make yourself and everyone around you absolutely nuts.

You have a need for harmony and balance in relationships. You dislike confrontation and dissension, so all too often you surrender to your partner's wants at your own expense. So which signs are good matches for you?

Gemini, Aquarius. Fellow air signs understand your psychological makeup. Gemini experiences some of the same duality that you do but for different reasons. He isn't bothered by dichotomies, since his own life is predicated on them. He appeals to that part of you that needs to communicate honestly. Aquarius may be a bit too rigid for you, insisting that you bend to his desires, but the depth and breadth of his vision attract you at a visceral level.

Sagittarius, Leo, Aries. Any of the fire signs could be an excellent match. Sagittarius never bores you and enjoys you for *who you are*. Leo may want more attention than you're willing to give, but her warmth and compassion will delight you. You and Aries, your opposite sign, balance each other.

Taurus, Virgo, Capricorn. Of the three earth signs, Taurus is probably the best match because you share Venus as a ruler. That means you have similar tastes in music and art and probably share some of the same attitudes and beliefs about money.

Creatively, Libras do well at music, art, writing—anything in the arts—but also excel with people.

Scorpio

As the most emotionally intense sign of the zodiac and one of the most psychic, your powerful and magnetic personality can intimidate even heads of state.

Your life patterns are about breaking taboos, digging deeper, looking for the absolute bottom line in whatever you do, in any relationship in which you become involved. You feel and intuit your way through life, and your partner must understand that.

All of this brooding and mulling takes place in the privacy of your own head. The side you show others is lighter, funny, with a dry wit that can charm, seduce, or spar with the best of them. Yet inside you're always asking, *What motivates him? What secrets does he have?* Given the complexities of your personality, which signs are most compatible with yours?

Pisces, Cancer. Of these two water signs, Pisces matches you in raw intuitive ability but may be too indecisive to suit you long term. Cancer can be just as secretive as you, but unless you've got a moon or rising in Cancer, this sign could be too clingy.

Taurus, Virgo, Capricorn. The earth signs are compatible matches. Taurus, your opposite sign, brings sensuality to your sexuality and helps to dispel your suspicions about other people's motives. Her earthiness grounds your psychic ability. Virgo's discerning and gentle nature mitigates your emotional intensity. Capricorn's determination appeals to that same quality in you.

Fire signs? *Leos* and Scorpios are both fixed signs, and there seems to be something between them that is powerful. Look at Leo Bill Clinton and Scorpio Hillary.

On the creative front, you're good at anything that enables you to use your intuition and your investigative skills.

Sagittarius

You're so multifaceted, with so many different talents, that a relationship presents certain dilemmas, e.g., commitment to another person. It's so much easier to commit to, well, your own interests! Also there's that little ole thing called personal freedom, which you value every bit as much as Aries.

Like Libra, there's a curious duality in your makeup, best explained perhaps by the symbol for your sign—the mythological centaur. Half horse, half human, this figure might be defined as the wild woman (or man) versus the conformist. A part of you operates from gut instinct and the other part of you is acculturated. Which signs are your best matches?

Aries, Leo, Sagittarius. As remarked under the Aries section, a relationship with this sign may not go anywhere because you're both so independent. Aries might want to be in charge all the time, and you get fed up and hit the open road. Leo could be a terrific choice, particularly if one of you has a moon in the other's sun sign. Another Sadge would be intriguing.

Taurus, Virgo, Capricorn. Of these three earth signs, Capricorn is the best match. Even if she lacks your intuitive gifts, her focus, direction, and resolute determination equal yours. Taurus, your opposite sign, could also be a good match. You share a fascination with the paranormal, and your energies would balance each other.

Air signs? Water signs? Probably not, unless you have a moon, rising, or some other prominent planet in those signs.

You would excel at anything creative that is related to travel, publishing, and higher education.

Capricorn

You build relationships in the same careful way that you build everything else in your life—a brick at a time. A conversation here, a dinner there, a movie, a moonlit walk, an exchange of beliefs: you're methodical, consistent, disciplined. Pretty soon the foundation is solid, the chemistry is exactly right, and you know exactly what you want.

A relationship, of course, involves the human heart—not mortar and bricks—and that's where it may get tricky. You could discover that your methodical approach doesn't work as well in a relationship as it does with your career. Your success will depend to a certain extent on your compatibility with your partner.

Taurus, Virgo, Capricorn. Taurus' solidity and dependability appeal to you, and he's as private as you are. But his still waters run deep, and he may not express his emotions as readily as you would like. Yet the match would be a good one. Virgo understands what drives you. Another Capricorn—i.e., type A personality—would wear you out!

Scorpio, Pisces. While either of these water signs is compatible with your earth-sign sun, Pisces may too ambivalent for you, too indecisive. Scorpio, though, is a strong match. All that intensity appeals to you at a visceral level, your sex life would be fantastic, and you share a similar determination. *Cancer*, your opposite sign, might work if the Cancer has a moon or rising in your sign.

Fire signs? Air signs? Again, it depends on the distribution of fire- and air-sign planets in your natal chart.

Your creative interests are varied, and you approach them with the same methodical, relentless energy that you bring to other facets of your life. You build worlds, Capricorn—in software, writing, photography, dance, art.

Aquarius

In love and romance, as in life, your mind is your haven, your sanctuary, your sacred place. It's where everything begins for you. From your visionary, cutting edge ideas to your humanitarian causes and interests in the esoteric, you're a wild card, not easily pigeonholed. It doesn't make any difference to you whether your partner shares these interests, as long as he or she recognizes your right to pursue them.

There's a rebel in you that pushes against the status quo, and that's something your partner has to understand too. Your connections to people and to the world aren't easily grasped by others. Too weird, they think. Too out there. But that's fine. You understand who and what you are, and in the end that's all you need. So which signs are your best matches?

Gemini, Libra. Your air-sign *compadres* are excellent matches. Gemini suits your prodigious intellect, causes, and ideas. Good communication usually is a hallmark of this relationship, and Gemini is supportive of your causes. With Libra the focus is on relationships—yours and Libra's connection to five million others. But the right mix exists for a strong partnership. A relationship with another *Aquarius* could be challenging since you'll both insist you're right. But if you can move past that, you'll do fine. Another Aquarius may be like looking in the mirror 24/7. Not for the faint hearted.

Aries, Leo, Sagittarius. With these fire signs you enjoy the freedom to be your own person. Life with Aries is never boring, the conversation and adventures are stimulating, but he may not share your humanitarian and esoteric interests. Sagittarius loves your mind and insights, your idealism and rebellion against the establishment. Great compatibility overall. Leo is your opposite sign, suggesting a good balance between your head and his heart.

Earth or water signs? Only if you have prominent planets in either of those elements.

Your creative talents don't fit under any tidy category. They are as varied and different as your lifestyle and worldview. If you focus on just one of these talents, you can mine it for gold!

Pisces

It's true that your inner world is often more real and genuine to you than anything in the external world. The richness of your imagination, the breadth of your intuition—these qualities create a kind of seductive atmosphere that's tough to move beyond. But because you're a physical being in a physical world, who has to eat and sleep, work and function, who loves and triumphs and yearns, you have to move beyond it. So you do.

But always there's an inner tension, a kind of bewilderment, a constant questioning. *Where am I going? What am I doing? Do I really want to do this or that?* Your head and your heart are forever at odds, so no wonder your sign is symbolized by two fish moving in opposite directions. In romance and love this indecisiveness can be problematic. So which signs are most compatible for you?

Scorpio, Cancer. Scorpio's emotional intensity could overwhelm you, but he balances your indecisiveness with his unwavering commitment to a particular path. Intuitively, you're on the same page, a major plus. Cancer's innate gentleness appeals to you, and she appreciates you exactly as you are.

Taurus, Capricorn. These two earth signs appeal to you at a visceral level. Taurus' solid, grounded personality comforts that part of you that is so often torn between one direction and another. Her sensuality is also a major plus. Capricorn's singular vision and direction are mysteries to you, but there's much to learn from her. *Virgo*, your opposite sign, can bring balance.

Fire signs probably won't work for you unless you have a moon or rising in a fire sign. Of the air signs, *Gemini* is probably the most compatible for you. Since you're both symbolized by two of something— two fish, the twins—he understands your dichotomies.

With your imagination and psychic ability, the world really lies at your feet in a creative sense. All you have to do is decide which talent to nurture and then plug yourself into it and let your muse do the rest.

♎ CHAPTER 4

Health and Fitness in 2013

Taking Responsibility for Your Own Health

In the U.S. more money per person is spent on health care than in any other country in the world. Yet life expectancy in this country ranks fiftieth, and the U.S. lags behind other wealthy nations in infant mortality. According to the Institute of Medicine, the United States is the only country in the world that doesn't ensure that all its citizens have coverage.

In the U.S. health insurance is controlled by private corporations whose bottom line is profit, not health. The only exceptions are government-run programs like Medicare, Medicaid, the Veterans' Administration, and some programs for children. If you followed the contentious health-care debate, you undoubtedly heard about death panels, government takeover of the health-care system, and other nonsense. One clip we remember was amusing: an older woman standing up at a Tea Party meeting, waving her sign—*No to Obama Care*—while she shouted, "Keep your hands off my Medicare!"

In the end, when the final bill went through Congress, there were some significant changes: mandated health insurance that begins in 2014, insurance companies can no longer deny coverage for preexisting conditions, and children can remain on their parents' health insurance until the age of twenty-six. But the bill didn't go far enough. Medicare for all would be the ideal.

Until insurance companies are removed from health care, the health care in this country will continue to be a discriminatory system. The real death panels will continue to be insurance companies who deny care for profit.

If nothing else, that debate and the reality of health care in this country should encourage you to take charge of your own health. Here are some simple suggestions:

1) *If you don't have a regular exercise routine yet, start one.* Pick something that you know you can do daily.

2) *Watch what you eat. Read the labels on the food you buy.* How much sodium is there in your favorite foods? How much cholesterol? Fats? Even organic foods have a high sodium content. The other day at Whole Foods we picked up some soy bacon and then turned the box over to look at the contents. For a single slice of soy bacon, the nutritional facts state:

Total fat—1 gram
No saturated or trans fat, no polyunsaturated or
   monounsaturated fats
Cholesterol—0 mg
Sodium—140 mg
Potassium—40 mg
No carbs, no sugar
Protein—2 g

That's a lot of sodium for a single skinny slice of soy bacon! Compare this to our favorite organic chicken sausage, however, which has 460 mg of sodium for a single link, and the soy bacon looks good. Once you get into the habit of reading the labels, you will be more careful in your selection of foods.

3) *Meditation and yoga are two healthy practices you might consider.* Meditation has been shown to: lower blood pressure and oxygen consumption, decrease respiratory rate, slow heart rate, reduce anxiety and stress, enhance the immune system. Yoga increases your physical flexibility—and eventually your emotional and mental flexibility as well. It helps to strengthen your body, improves muscle tone, improves posture, improves lung capacity because of the deep breathing involved, and reduces stress.

4) *Try various nutritional and vitamin programs.* Educate yourself. The Internet is filled with health and fitness Web sites.

5) *Try a homeopathic practitioner or acupuncturist before you run to your doctor for a prescription.*

If you were an alien watching the evening news and the drug commercials that sponsor it, you might get the impression that Americans are a sickly lot in search of the quickest fix. While drugs certainly have their place, more and more Americans are seeking alternative treatments for whatever ails them. From acupuncture to yoga and homeopathy, from vitamin regimens to nutritional programs, more and more of us are taking control over our own health and bodies.

6) *Take inventory of your beliefs.* If medical intuitives like Louise Hay and Carolyn Myss are correct, then our health is about more than just eating right

and getting sufficient exercise. It's also about our emotions, our inner worlds, our belief systems. How happy are you in your job? Your closest partnerships? Your friendships? Are you generally happy with the money you earn? What would you change about your life? Do you believe you have free will or that everything is destined? Is your mood generally upbeat? Do you feel you have choices? Do you feel empowered? By asking yourself these kinds of questions, you can glean a sense of your emotional state at any given time. And the state of your emotions may tell you a great deal about the state of your health.

Louise Hay, author of *You Can Heal Your Life* and founder of Hay House publishing, is a living testament to the impact of emotions on health. As a young woman she was diagnosed with vaginal cancer. The doctors wanted to operate, but Hay bought herself time — three months — by telling them she didn't have the money. She then took control of her treatment.

As a child who had been sexually abused at the age of five, it wasn't surprising to her that the cancer had shown up where it had. She knew that cancer was "a dis-ease of deep resentment that has been held for a long period of time until it literally eats away at the body." She felt that if she could change the mental pattern that had created the cancer, if she could release the patterns of resentment, then she could cure herself.

She set out a program for her treatment, and forgiveness was the top of her list. She also knew she had to "love and approve" of herself more. In addition she found a good therapist, nutritionist, and foot reflexologist, had colonics three times a week, and exercised. Her treatment is spelled out in her book. The end result? Within six months the doctors pronounced her free of cancer.

In her book there's an invaluable list: next to every ailment and disease is the probable emotional cause and the new thought pattern that will lead to healing. Her techniques may not be for everyone, but when dealing with health and fitness issues remember that medical science doesn't have all the answers, and you, in fact, may be your own best healer.

7) *Practice the art of appreciation. Expect the best from others.* If you can get into the habit of doing these two things, you're well ahead of the game in maintaining your health.

The Physical You

These descriptions fit both sun and rising signs. For a more complete look at the physical you, of course, your entire natal chart should be taken into account, with a particularly close look at the sign of your moon—the root of your emotions, the cradle of your inner world.

Aries

Rules: head and face

2013 Tip:

In this year of transformation transform yourself from the inside out, Aries. Start with your thoughts. Notice what you think throughout a given day. If you notice that a lot of negative thoughts surface, nudge them on their way by reaching for more positive ones.

Health and Fitness

Aries rules the head and face, so these areas are often the most vulnerable physically. Headaches, dizziness, and skin eruptions can be common. If you're an athletic Aries, then do more of whatever it is that you enjoy. Competitive sports? Great, go for it. Long-distance runner? Run farther. Gym? Double your time and your workout. Yoga once a week? Do it three times a week. One way or another you need to burn off your excessive energy, so that it doesn't turn inward and short-circuit your body!

As a cardinal fire sign you're an active person who gravitates toward daring, risky sports—mountain climbing, rappelling, bungee jumping, trekking through high mountainous regions, leaping out of airplanes. It's probably a great idea to have good health insurance or a Louise Hay attitude toward your health—*I'm attracting only magnificent experiences into my life.*

For maximum benefit you probably should try to eliminate red meat from your diet. Chicken and fish are fine, but a vegan diet would be best. Herbs like mustard, eye-bright, and bay are beneficial for you. Any antioxidant is helpful—particularly vitamins C, E, A or Lutein for your eyes, zinc, Co-Q10, Black Co-hosh if you're a female in menopause, or Saw Palmetto if you're a man older than fifty. If you pull a muscle or throw your back out of whack, look for a good acupuncturist and avoid painkillers.

Taurus

Rules: neck, throat, cervical vertebrae

2013 Tip:

Since this is a year of transformation, start by communicating what you feel to someone you love. Don't take it for granted that the person knows how you feel.

Health and Fitness

Thanks to the sensuality of your sign, you may be a gourmet cook and enjoy rich foods. But because your metabolism may be somewhat slow, you benefit from daily exercise and moderation in your diet. In fact, moderation in all things is probably a good rule to follow.

As a fixed earth sign you benefit from any outdoor activity, and the more physical it is, the better it is for you. Hiking, skiing, windsurfing, biking are all excellent pursuits. You also benefit from any mind/body discipline like tai chi or yoga. The latter is especially good since it keeps you flexible, and that flexibility spills over into your attitudes and beliefs and the way you deal with situations and people. You probably enjoy puttering in a garden, but because you have such an artistic side, you don't just putter. You remake the garden into a work of art—fountains, bold colors, mysterious paths that twist through greenery and flowers. Once you include wind chimes and bird feeders, nature's music adds the finishing touches.

If your job entails long hours of sitting in front of a computer, your neck and shoulders may be more tense than usual. You would benefit through regular massage and hot tub soaks.

If you're the silent type of Taurus, then chances are you don't discuss your emotions. This tendency can cause health challenges if you keep anger or resentment bottled up inside you. Best to have an outlet — exercise, for example, or some sort of creative endeavor. Art, music, photography, writing: any of those would help. Better yet, learn to open up with at least one or two people!

Gemini

Rules: hands, arms, lungs, nervous system

2013 Tip:

Begin your year of transformation by focusing on one area of your life that you would like to improve, to clean up. You often tend to spread yourself too thin, so the focus will benefit you.

Health and Fitness

You benefit from periodic breaks in your established routine. Whether it's a trip to some exotic port or the grocery, it's a breath of fresh air, a way to hit the pause button on your busy mind. Regular physical exercise helps to bleed off some of your energy and keeps your already youthful body supple and in shape.

As a mutable air sign you need intellectual stimulation and a constant array of experiences and information that keep your curiosity piqued. Otherwise it's too easy for all that nervous energy to turn inward and affect your health. The kind of work you do is important in the overall scheme of your health. You do best in nonroutine kinds of work with flexible hours or preferably in a profession where you make your own hours! Any job in communication, travel, public relations would suit you. When you're passionate about what you do, you're happier. If you're happy, your immune system remains healthy.

With your natural dexterity and coordination, you would do well at yoga. If you don't take classes yet, sign up for some. Not only will it keep you flexible, but you'll benefit mentally. Meditation would also be an excellent practice for you. Anything to calm your busy head!

Since your respiratory and nervous systems are your most vulnerable areas, your diet should include plenty of fish, fresh fruits, and vegetables. If you live in a place where you can garden, plant some of these items for optimum freshness. Vitamin C, zinc, the B vitamins, and vitamins E and A are also beneficial for you. With your energy always in fast-forward, it's smart to get at least seven or preferably eight hours of sleep a night. If you're the type of Gemini with a high metabolism, then you benefit from eating several small meals throughout the day rather than just the usual three.

Cancer

Rules: breasts, stomach, digestive system

2013 Tip:

During this year of transformation step out of your subjective universe and try to see the world through someone else's eyes. Zip yourself up in another's skin.

Health and Fitness

As a cardinal water sign you benefit from proximity to water. If you can live or work close to a body of water, you'll notice a marked difference in your energy and intuition and how you feel and think. Even a vacation close to the water is healing. This seems to hold true not only for Cancer sun signs, but for moon and rising signs in Cancer too. The body of water can be anything—a lake, river, ocean, salt marsh, even a pond!

Not surprisingly, you benefit from any kind of water sport, even a day at the beach or a picnic by the river. The point is that water speaks to you. It feels like your natural element. You might want to read *The Secret of Water* or any of the other books by Masaru Emoto. You will never think of water in the same way again and will be more conscious of how human emotions affect water—and thus our bodies, since we consist of nearly 70 percent water.

Emotionally, you may cling to past injuries and hurts more than other signs or may still be dragging around issues from childhood or even from a past life. Unresolved emotional stuff can lodge in your body and create problems. So it's important that you rid yourself of past resentments and anger. Use hypnosis to dislodge these feelings. Forgive and forget. Have a past-life regression. Read Louise Hay's book, *You Can Heal Your Life.*

If you have a moon, rising, or another planet in an earth sign, consider regular workouts at a gym.

Leo

Rules: heart, back, spinal cord

2013 Tip:

For the year of transformation promise yourself there will be a minimum of drama in your personal life. Whenever you feel yourself at the brink of an emotional outburst or meltdown, detach, step back.

Health and Fitness

Leo rules the heart. So you benefit from a low-fat diet, exercise, work that you love, and relationships in which you are recognized as the unique person that you are. Yes, those last two things count in the overall picture of your health!

Let's talk about your work. Acting, of course, is what you're known for. And performance. And politics. And, well, anything where you can show off your abundant talents. So if right now you're locked into a humdrum job, low person on the bureaucratic totem pole, and don't receive the attention you feel you deserve, then your pride and ambition are suffering. That in turn creates resentment that could be eating you alive. Turn the situation around by finding a career or an outlet where your talents shine and you're appreciated and recognized. You're a natural leader whose flamboyant style and magnetism attract the supporters who can help you.

You have a temper, but once you blow, that's it. Unlike Cancer, you don't hold on to grudges or harbor resentments or anger from childhood. You tend to be forward looking in your outlook, and your natural optimism is healthy for your heart and immune system. Anything you can do to maintain your cheerful disposition is a plus. When you feel yourself getting down, rent comedies, find books that make you laugh out loud, blog about your feelings.

Virgo

Rules: intestines, abdomen, female reproductive system

2013 Tip:

Since this is the year of transformation, be as detailed and specific as possible about an exercise routine. If you go to the gym three days a week, extend it to four or five days. If you take yoga once a week, try doing it twice a week. If you meditate five minutes a day, go for ten minutes.

Health and Fitness

If you're the type of Virgo who worries and frets a lot, then the first place it's likely to show up is in your digestive tract. You might have colic as an infant, stomach upsets as a teenager, ulcers as an adult. The best way to mitigate this tendency, of course, is to learn how NOT to worry and to simply go with the flow.

You do best on a diet that includes plenty of fresh fruits and vegetables, fish, and chicken. Try to stay away from fried or heavily spiced foods. Red meat might be difficult to digest. If you live in a place where fresh fruits and vegetables are difficult to find during the winter, then supplement your diet with the appropriate vitamins and minerals. If you're a fussy eater—and some Virgos are—then the vitamin and mineral supplements are even more important.

You benefit from hot baths, massages, anything that allows you to relax into the moment. Yoga, running, swimming, gym workouts—any of these exercise regimens benefits you. Some Virgos, particularly double Virgos—with a moon or rising in that sign—have an acute sense of smell. If you're one of those, then be sure to treat yourself to scented soaps and lotions, fragrant candles and incense, and any other scent that soothes your soul.

Virgo is typically associated with service, and you may find that whenever you do a good deed for someone, when you volunteer your time or expertise, you feel better about yourself and life in general. The more you can do to trigger these feelings, the healthier you'll be. You have a tendency toward self-criticism that's part and parcel of your need for perfection, and whenever you find yourself shifting into that critical frame of mind, stop it in its tracks. Reach for a more uplifting thought. This will help you to maintain your health.

Libra

Rules: lower back, kidney, diaphragm

2013 Tip:

You're always seeking the very thing that probably eludes you: balance. So during this year of transformation, be as independent as you can. Put yourself first. Do what *you* enjoy.

Health and Fitness

If your love life is terrific, your health probably is, too. You're happiest when you're in a relationship, preferably a committed, lifetime relationship. When things between you and your partner are on an even keel, your energy is greater, your immune system works without a hitch, you sleep more soundly, and you're more apt to have a healthier lifestyle.

You prefer working in an environment that's aesthetically pleasing, where there's a minimum of drama, and with congenial people. If your work situation doesn't fit that description, it could affect your health—and for the same reasons as a love life that is lacking. Emotions. Your lower back, kidneys, and diaphragm are vulnerable areas for you, and unvented emotions could manifest in those areas first. If it isn't possible to change jobs or careers right now, then find an artistic outlet for your creative expression. Music, photography, art, writing, dance, any area that allows you to flex your creativity.

You benefit from yoga, walking, swimming, and any kind of exercise that strengthens your lower-back muscles. Meditation is also beneficial, particularly when it's combined with an awareness of breathing.

The healthiest diet for you should consist of foods with varied tastes, plenty of fresh fruits and vegetables—organic if possible—and a minimum of meats. Anything that benefits your kidneys is good. Drink at least eight glasses of water a day, so that your kidneys are continually flushed out.

Scorpio

Rules: sexual organs, elimination

2013 Tip:

In this year of transformation, a process you understand well, allow your considerable intuition to guide you in all matters, including your health.

Health and Fitness

As a fixed water sign you probably benefit by a proximity to water every bit as much as Cancer does. Lake, ocean, river, pond, salt marsh: take your pick. If none of these is available, put a fountain in your backyard or somewhere in your house and create a meditation area. It's important that you have a quiet center where you can decompress at the end of the day, particularly if you have a busy family life and a lot of demands on your time.

You tend to keep a lot of emotion locked inside, and if the emotions are negative—resentment, anger—they fester and affect your health. So try to find someone you can talk to freely about your emotions—a partner, friend, family member. Or pour these feelings into a creative outlet. One way or another, get them out.

Scorpio rules the sexual and elimination organs, so these areas could be where ill health hits first. Be sure that you eat plenty of roughage and enjoy what you eat while you're eating it. Stay away from the usual culprits—fried or heavily processed foods. You do best with plenty of fresh food but may want to consider eliminating red meats. Consider colonics treatments for cleaning out the bowels.

For your overall health it's important to enjoy sex with a partner whom you trust. Avoid using sex as a leverage for power in a relationship.

Sagittarius

Rules: hips, thighs, liver

2013 Tip:

To keep yourself really healthy in this year of transformation, attend to details—emotional, physical, intellectual, and spiritual. Be precise.

Health and Fitness

As a mutable fire sign you can't tolerate any kind of restriction or limitation on your freedom. You must be able to get up and go whenever you want. If you work in a job that demands you punch a time clock and your hours are strictly regulated, or are in a relationship where you feel constricted, then you probably aren't happy. For a naturally buoyant and happy person like you, that could spell health challenges. Sadge rules the hips, sacral region of the spine, coccygeal vertebrae, femur, ileum, iliac arteries, and sciatic nerves, so any of these areas could be impacted health-wise.

You benefit from any kind of athletic activity. From competitive sports to an exercise regimen you create, your body craves regular activity. You also benefit from yoga, which keeps your spine and hips flexible.

If you're prone to putting on weight—and even if

you're not!—strive to minimize sweets and carbs in your diet. The usual recommendations—abundant fresh vegetables and fruits—also apply. If you're the type who eats on the run, then you may be eating fast or heavily processed foods and should try to keep that at a minimum or eliminate it altogether. Even though your digestive system is hard enough to tolerate just about anything, the fast foods and processed foods add carbs and calories.

Antioxidants are beneficial, of course, and these include vitamins C, A, and E. Minerals like zinc should be included in your diet and also a glucosamine supplement for joints.

Capricorn

Rules: knees, skin, bones

2013 Tip:

During this year of transformation ease up on yourself. You tend to be quite the workaholic, and it's okay to back off for a while, to give yourself a break, dive into a creative venture for the sheer joy of it.

Health and Fitness

Since you seem to have been born with an innate sense of where you're going—or want to go—it's likely that you take care of yourself. You know the routine as well as anyone—eat right, stay fit, exercise, get enough rest. But there are other components to living long and prospering (to paraphrase Spock!), and that's your emotions.

You, like Scorpio, are secretive, although your motives are different. For you it's a privacy factor more than anything else. You keep your emotions to yourself and may not express what you feel when you feel it. This can create blockages in your body, notably in your joints or knees. It's vital that you learn to vent your emotions, to rid yourself of anger before it has a chance to move inward.

You're focused, ambitious, and patient in the attainment of your goals. But your work—your satisfaction with it—is a primary component in your health. If you feel you've reached a dead end in your career, if you're frustrated more often than you're happy with what you do, then it's time to revamp and get out of Dodge. By taking clear, definite steps toward something else, you feel you're more in control of your destiny and mitigate the possibility of health challenges.

Since your knees are vulnerable, running is probably not the best form of exercise for you, unless you do it only once or twice a week and engage in some other form of exercise the rest of the time. For a cardio workout that isn't as tough on your knees, try a rowing machine. For general flexibility, there's nothing like yoga!

Aquarius

Rules: ankles, shins, circulatory system

2013 Tip:

For this year, Aquarius, develop your intuition. Attend a workshop in intuitive development. Experiment with various divination systems. Learn to read the signs and symbols in your life.

Health and Fitness

Let's start with the effect of Uranus ruling your sign. It sometimes can set your nerves on edge—too many sounds, too much chaos around you, loud noises deep into the night, the backfiring of cars, the incessant drone of traffic, even a crowd at the local mall. You're sensitive to all of that. It's part of what makes it important for you to have a private space to which you can withdraw—a quiet backyard filled with plants, a room inside your house with an altar for your Wiccan practice, filled with scents from candles or incense that soothe your frazzled nerves. Or perhaps a book on tape can shut it all out. But shut it out you must to protect your health.

Because you live so much inside your own head, exercise is definitely beneficial for you. It doesn't have to be anything complicated—yoga done in the privacy of your own home, long walks, regular bike rides. But do *something* to ground your body, to get your blood moving, to silence the buzz inside your head. It will all benefit your health.

Nutrition? Well, for an Aquarius, this can go any number of different ways. You enjoy different types of food, so that's a place to start—with what you *enjoy*. The foods are likely to be unusual—organically grown, for instance, prepared in unusual ways, or purchased from a local co-op. If you live in the city, perhaps you purchase food from a grocery store you've been frequenting for years. The idea here is that *you* know what's best for your body, what you can tolerate, what you need. Even though Aquarians aren't generally as in touch with their bodies as earth signs, they have an intuitive sense about what works for them. In the end that's all that matters.

Pisces

Rules: the feet, is associated with the lymphatic system

2013 Tip:

Treat yourself to a weekend at a spa. Pamper yourself. In this year of transformation bestow on yourself the attention you usually shower on others.

Health and Fitness

Let's start with emotions. Let's start with the fact that you're a psychic sponge, able to absorb other people's moods and thoughts with the ease of a magnet attracting every other piece of metal around it. Yes, let's start there. It's why you should associate only with optimistic, upbeat people. The negative types steal your energy, wreck your immune system, and leave you in a tearful mess at the end of the rainbow with nothing to show for your journey.

Like your fellow water signs Cancer and Scorpio, you probably benefit from proximity to water. Whether you live near water, work near it, or vacation near it, water refreshes your soul, spirit, intuition, and your immune system. Read Masaru Emoto's books on how water responds to emotions and intent. You'll never think about water in the same way again. You'll never think about your sun sign in the same way again either.

You benefit from any kind of exercise, but try something that speaks to your soul. Swimming. Rowing, but in an actual boat, on an actual river instead of in a gym. Even a hot tub where you kick your legs is beneficial. Pay attention to the water you drink. Is your tap water filled with fluorides? Then avoid it and look for distilled water. Drink at least eight glasses a day. Indulge yourself in massages, foot reflexology, periodic dips in the ocean. Any ocean.

CHAPTER 5

You and Your Money in 2013

Right now, in early 2011, signs of the recession that started in 2007 are still painfully evident. In August 2010, for instance, nearly 15 million people remained unemployed, and the unemployment rate was just under 10 percent. In some areas of the country—Michigan, for instance—the unemployment rate is higher.

According to an article from the AP in mid-September 2010, more homes were foreclosed in August 2010 than at any point during the mortgage crisis—95,364, to be exact. RealtyTrac's figures are staggering: since 2007 more than 2.3 million homes have been foreclosed. As of September 16, 2010, CNBC reported that the states with the highest foreclosure rates were, in descending order: Hawaii, Illinois, Michigan, Georgia, Utah, Idaho, California, Arizona, Florida, and Nevada.

These figures point to a troubling pattern that has been prevalent throughout the early twenty-first century—greed. Whether it's corporate or individual greed, there are no free rides. Banks lent to people who didn't have the income to meet mortgage payments, bundled good and bad mortgages together, and sold them off. Borrowers used their homes as ATM machines. In a sense what is happening to the American economy is a reflection of what has happened to the U.S. economy overall: we are living beyond our means. Right now the U.S. debt stands at more than $13 trillion. In fact, you can check the debt, live, right here: http://www.brillig.com/debt_clock

So what do all these depressing statistics mean for you in 2013? Well, you may be taking a deeper look this year at your financial picture—and your attitudes and beliefs about money. Are you a risk-taker? Do you stash away a percentage of everything you make? Do you spend money as quickly as it comes in? Do you have a realistic budget? Are you in credit-card debt? Do you live debt free? Depending on your financial situation, here are tips for each sign on how to maximize your potential this year; when the stars favor your finances—and when they don't.

But first take this inventory about your beliefs concerning money.

Belief Inventory

Here's a list of some commonly held negative beliefs about money. Check the ones to which you subscribe:

- Money is the root of all evil.
- Money is nonspiritual.
- The rich have major problems in their lives.
- Money corrupts.

- If you have too much money, you have to worry about losing it.
- If you have too much money, it takes over your life.
- The wealthy don't have money problems, but they have a lot of other problems.

You get the idea here. Many of these beliefs we've adopted from family and peers and have held on to them because they're comfortable, we believe they're true, or because we don't even realize we believe them! So if you're not satisfied with what you're earning, start monitoring how you think about money. Any time you find yourself thinking a negative thought about money, turn the thought around by thinking something more positive. Also, read Napoleon Hills' classic *Think and Grow Rich* and *Money and the Law of Attraction* by Esther and Jerry Hicks.

Now let's take a look at how you can maximize your earning potential in 2013.

Aries

You fall into several distinct types. One type is an impulsive spender: you see something you like, whip out the plastic, and buy it. Then you suffer the next month when that bill comes due, along with all your other bills. Then there's another type of Aries, who saves for something special—a trip, an appliance, a car—but isn't saving long range. Another type saves with the distant future in mind. Which type do you fit into?

There are two excellent periods this year for finances. The first period falls between March 21 and

April 15, when Venus is in your sign. This period is excellent for earning additional money for sales, asking for a raise. The second period, when Venus transits Taurus and your financial area, falls between April 15 and May 9. During this period you may be more prone toward saving rather than spending. But if you do feel the urge to spend, it may be for high-end items—art, jewelry. So if you succumb to the urge, be sure to pay cash!

Although we talk about Jupiter transits in a later chapter, this planet's transit through Gemini could be quite nice for your finances. That time frame: January 1 to June 25. Excellent backup dates: March 12 to April 20, when Mars transits your sign.

Taurus

As a fixed earth sign you're more the saving than the spending type. That said, you enjoy your creature comforts and can be easily seduced by big-ticket items—art, jewelry, that top-of-the-line mountain bike, a yoga retreat in Costa Rica. One thing you enjoy is good food. Your palate is well developed, and there isn't much that you won't eat. But food is really special when it's exotic, so one of your main expenses may be restaurants!

An excellent time this year for maximizing your earning potential falls between April 15 and May 9, when Venus is in your sign. This period is one in which you feel extremely good about yourself and life in general, and that feeling bolsters your self-confidence. Others pick up on this, and suddenly, Taurus, you can do no wrong. You get hired for that job you want, you land a promotion or raise, you sell your novel.

The next period that could pay off financially falls between June 25, 2013, and July 16, 2014, when Jupiter transits Cancer, a water sign compatible with your earth-sign sun. This occurs in your solar third house of communication and travel. Perhaps this would be a good time to dust off that old manuscript. Or perhaps there's a new gold mine awaiting you in travel!

Good backup dates: April 20 to May 31, when Mars transits your sign. This one kicks butt, Taurus.

Gemini

Left to your own devices, you think things like checkbooks and saving accounts, IRAs and investments, are for other people to ponder—like your accountant, partner, parents, sibling. You would rather write and talk about *ideas*. So let's talk about the *idea* of money. What does it actually represent to you? Energy? Freedom? Albatross? During this year of transformation it's to your advantage to look at money as energy and freedom. The more you make, the greater your freedom to do what interests you. The more effort you expend, the greater the energy you're putting into what you do and the greater the return. At least that's how it's supposed to work in theory. But you have to remain focused, resolute.

One of your best times this year for increasing your earnings falls between January 1 and June 25, when expansive Jupiter transits your sign. This transit has been going on since 2012, so by now you should have a clear idea how it works and the kind of luck and expansion that accompanies it. Another excellent period for increasing your earnings occurs between May

9 and June 2, when Venus transits your sign and travels with Jupiter. Things may seem to be going so well that you could be tempted to kick back and chill. Resist that temptation! Use this time frame to move forward—ask for a raise, apply for a promotion, look for a new job that pays more.

Another favorable financial period occurs between May 9 and June 2, when Venus transits your sign. This transit should be good for you financially and otherwise. You have such appeal now that it's easy for you to get the job you apply for or land that raise, that promotion, that big sale. Believe it—and watch it happen.

An excellent backup period is May 31 to July 13, when Mars transits your sign. It propels you toward what you desire.

Cancer

You probably do well budgeting your money. In fact you probably know exactly what you earn, what you spend, and on what. You're not obsessed with money, but you recognize that you spend at least forty hours a week earning your living, so it makes sense to keep track of your finances. You tend to be a saver, not just for the short term but for the long term as well.

This year there are several periods that favor your finances. The first occurs between June 2 and 27, when Venus transits your sign. During this period ask for a raise or promotion, apply for new jobs, network with professional peers, open an IRA. Keep in mind, though, that Mercury is retrograde in your sign between June 26 and July 20, so just to be safe confine the above suggestions to June 2 to 25!

The second period when your finances—and just about everything else in your life—may undergo radical expansion occurs between June 25, 2013, and July 16, 2014. Jupiter transits your sign during this period, and what a treat it should be for you, Cancer. You'll feel as if you're in the right place at the right time, that the sky is literally the limit. An excellent backup period occurs between July 13 and August 27, when Mars is in your sign. This transit acts like a booster rocket, and it shouts, *Go for it!*

Leo

Your flamboyance and flair for drama probably translate into expenses for clothing, home furnishings, cars, jewelry, and anything else that catches your eye. It's not that you're constantly on the prowl for these expensive items, simply that when you spend money, this is where it goes. If you make a great deal of money, then it's not a problem. But if you're supporting a family, have a child in college, a mortgage, or a middle-class income, it could be a challenge.

Your first step, then, is inventory. Take a look at how much you make and deduct the taxes and FICA that you pay and anything else that is deducted automatically from your pay. That figure is what you actually earn in hard cash. Now take a look at your monthly expenses. How much money is left over after you pay those expenses?

There are some good times in 2013 for increasing your earnings. The first period falls between June 27 and July 22, when Venus transits your sign. This one really boosts self-confidence, other people find you infinitely appealing, and you can do no wrong, Leo. So ask for a raise or promotion, send out résumés. Unexpected bonuses or royalties could arrive during this time. If so, stash the money in an IRA.

The next period falls between January 1 and June 25, when Jupiter transits compatible air sign Gemini. Luck and expansion, Leo! This can be applied to any area of your life.

Virgo

You're the most discriminating of signs, measured, deliberate, with a penchant for details. You can be something of a perfectionist too, but rarely demand of others what you demand of yourself. Whatever you take on, you do so with complete dedication. So in 2013 perfect your finances, Virgo. Set your monetary goal, then figure out how best to achieve it.

One of the most favorable periods for earning more falls between July 22 and August 16, when Venus transits your sign. This period is favorable for landing a raise or promotion, receiving money from unexpected sources—an insurance payment, a royalty check—and sending out résumés for a job that pays you more. It's good for pitching manuscripts and screenplays.

Another potentially profitable period occurs between June 25, 2013, and July 16, 2014, when Jupiter transits compatible water sign Cancer and forms a beneficial angle to your sun. This period is when you're in the right place at the right time to bolster your bank account, land a raise, or make money by expanding your services or products to overseas markets.

Excellent backup dates: October 15 to December 7,

when Mars is in your sign. Think of this transit as your booster rocket.

Libra

Like Taurus, the other Venus-ruled sign, you enjoy being surrounded by beauty. Chances are that some of your disposable income goes toward art, jewelry, flowers, beautiful furniture—like a piano?—or perhaps toward some idiosyncratic collection you have. You can certainly save when you want to, though, and in this year of transformation it's smart to have a buffer.

Even if you earn more money this year, Libra, and you probably will, stash away a fixed percentage. Put it in an IRA or savings account, or simply take the cash and hide it somewhere! Between August 16 and September 11 Venus, your ruler, transits your sign. This period should be particularly good for you. Venus is happy in your sign and can help you to bring in additional income from a variety of different sources. If you're in sales, then you can sell anything to anyone. You might sell a manuscript, piece of art, or some other product born of your creativity.

During Jupiter's transit of fellow air sign Gemini between January 1 and June 25 you may experience an expansion in your income that seems to happen without any effort on your part. That's an illusion, of course. You have been seeding the possibilities for quite a while now. Excellent backup dates: December 7 to July 26, when Mars is in your sign. This long transit is due to a retrograde between March 1 and May 20, 2014. But while Mars is moving direct, it's your best friend, your booster rocket!

Scorpio

You're no stranger to transformation. With Pluto as the ruler of your sign, your life is constantly undergoing transformation of some kind. But if you would like to transform your finances, then 2013 is the year for you to seize the reins, Scorpio, and make things happen. Your considerable intuition and ability to get to the absolute bottom line of anything you research and investigate serve you well this year.

Between September 11 and October 7 Venus transits your sign. So during this period ask for a raise, apply for a promotion, send out résumés for jobs that really interest you. Be proactive. You and your ideas appeal to others. Another excellent period for expanding your income occurs between June 25, 2013, and July 16, 2014, when Jupiter transits fellow water sign Cancer and forms a beneficial angle to your sun. This period should be productive for you, with new creative opportunities that could bring in additional income.

Saturn begins the year in your sign, Scorpio, which could cause some delays or restrictions in your life. It's important that you meet your responsibilities and obligations so that Saturn's energies work to create solid financial foundations for you.

Sagittarius

Let the good times roll . . . and roll! As a mutable fire sign your life is about activity and forward motion. You don't have time for things like budgets, balancing a checkbook, keeping track of what you earn and spend. Then when it's time to do your taxes, you freak out. You can't find receipts, your files are messed up— you get the idea. So this year, Sadge, make organization of your finances one of your priorities. Once you've done that, you can receive the full benefit of several opportune times for increasing your income. More money means more travel, and if you're like most Sadges, travel feeds your nomadic soul.

Between October 7 and November 5 Venus transits your sign. Not only does your self-confidence soar, but others find you appealing and want you on their team. So ask for a raise or promotion, pitch your ideas, submit your manuscript or screenplay or some other product you have created.

Between January 1 and June 25 Jupiter transits Gemini, your opposite sign. During this period your professional partnerships expand, and that expansion could be a big boost to you financially.

Capricorn

As a cardinal earth sign you build your financial world just as you do everything else—one brick at a time. You do it patiently and methodically and usually have a goal in mind—double your earnings in six months, for instance. Or pay off your mortgage in the next two years.

In 2013 you have several windows of opportunity when it's easier to increase your earnings, launch a business, pitch an idea that someone will buy, sell a book. Luck is on your side, you're in the right place at the right time, you meet exactly the right people who make things happen. The first period falls between January 9 and February 1, when Venus is in your sign.

This transit is a confidence booster. When you feel good about yourself, others pick up on it, and suddenly everything flows your way. If you're looking for a better-paying job or a second job, then this period could bring news.

The second period occurs between June 25, 2013, and July 16, 2014, when Jupiter transits your opposite sign, Cancer. This transit should expand your professional partnerships, which in turn could be very positive for your finances.

You have an additional plus this year. Saturn is in Scorpio, forming a strong and beneficial angle to your sun. This transit helps you to build solid financial foundations.

Aquarius

You don't really fit into any financial category. Some Aquarius are great with money, others aren't. Some are savers, others are spenders. But one thing is for sure. When you make up your mind to do something, you do it. No one and nothing can sway you from a path you've chosen. So in this year of transformation let's look at times when your income can increase.

One of the most favorable periods falls between February 1 and 25. Venus transits your sign, so your appeal is broad, and others like you and your ideas, making this an ideal time to ask for a raise. Ask with the expectation that the raise will be given. Whether you're sending out résumés or interviewing for jobs, you're in your element and should reap the rewards you so justly deserve.

Another good period for you falls between January

1 and June 25, when Jupiter transits fellow air sign Gemini. This transit has been going on since 2012, so you probably have noticed the kinds of gifts it can bring. Follow the signs and synchronicities, Aquarius. During this period you're in the right place at the right time.

Pisces

Your considerable imagination and intuition will prove enormously valuable in this year of transformation. Whatever you can imagine, after all, can manifest itself. So if you're imagining a quantum leap in your income, Pisces, fix a figure firmly in mind, focus on it, release it—and let the universe figure out the connections that must be made for you to earn that amount of money.

In the interim, of course, it's smart not to just sit back, but to become more proactive. If you dislike your job, then figure out what you would like to be doing and start submitting applications and résumés. If you often find yourself short of money, set up a realistic budget and try to stick to it. You know, do the small stuff!

Timing is essential, so let's take a look at the windows of opportunity in 2013 when things really flow your way. These periods are when you should ask for a raise or promotion, submit résumés, schedule interviews, do whatever you can to earn more. The first period falls between February 25 and March 21, when Venus transits your sign. This is when you're more you than ever! Turn on the charm; let your muse in 24/7. The second period is lengthy—June 25, 2013, to July 16, 2014. Jupiter transits fellow water sign Cancer and forms a beneficial angle to your sun. Expansion, luck, you're in the right place at the right time!

CHAPTER 6

Career Choices in 2013

At the pinnacle of the Great Depression in 1933 almost 25 percent of the nation's work force—nearly 13 million people—was unemployed. As of late October 2011 unemployment in the U.S. hovered just under 10 percent, with nearly 15 million people unemployed. Lower percentage, but more people. However, in the Great Depression, the social safety nets were missing—unemployment insurance, Social Security, Medicare, Medicaid, food stamps, and other welfare programs. Also, thanks to technological advances, the variety of available jobs is broader than it was in the 1930s.

So despite all the grim statistics, many people flourish financially during difficult times. How can you be one of them? If you've been laid off from your job, the first thing you can do to turn things around is to look at it as an opportunity. Take stock of your talents and passions. What would you most enjoy doing? Is there a way you can turn your passions into a moneymaker?

Maybe you've always wanted to work with animals

in some capacity. If so, volunteer at your local animal shelter or at a private animal rescue center. With a little luck, determination, and focus, you might be able to turn it into a full-time job. Or, if you were going to start a business, what sort of business would it be? Do your market research and determine if there's a niche that your service or talent could fill.

The more positive and upbeat your attitude, the more frequently you view every challenge as an opportunity, the greater the chances that you'll turn things around.

Several years ago friends of ours, a married couple who are both writers, had pretty much hit rock bottom. The wife admitted that she was ready to start cleaning pools just to have a steady income. Then practically overnight everything turned around. Her husband sold a novel that became a popular cable-TV show; a producer commissioned her to write a script. Suddenly their bank account fattened, they bought a second home, new car, and boat, and the world opened up for them. It can open up for you too.

We create our realities from the inside out. Everything you see around you is a manifestation of a belief that you hold. Some of our beliefs have been passed down to us by well-meaning family members, mentors, teachers, or friends, and we adopt those beliefs because we respect the people who handed them to us. But what do *you* believe about your abilities and talents and your ability to earn your living doing what you love? How do you handle stress? Change?

In 2013 when so much of the world seems to be shifting beneath our feet, we have a chance to delve into those beliefs and get rid of the ones we have adopted out of convenience. We can either go with the flow, change with the times, or offer up resistance. The more we resist, the more pain we experience. The more we go with the flow, the greater our capacity to discover where we should be. Which path will you take?

Inventory

One way to prosper professionally during good *and* bad times is to know what you want. So let's take an inventory.

1. What is your dream job/profession? Describe it. Be detailed.

_____

_____

_____

2. How can you attain this dream job/profession? Do you need more education, time, additional skills? If so, include those things, and set a goal for attaining them.

_____

_____

_____

3. Set realistic professional goals. Choose a time frame—a month, six months, a year, whatever feels right to you. Ask yourself what you would like to

be doing a year from now. Describe it in detail.
Make it real!

_____

_____

_____

4. Inner work is just as important as the external
   steps you take to realize a goal. You might, for example, start meditating as a way to ground yourself
   and mitigate any stress you're experiencing. Or
   perhaps you start using visualization daily to help
   you to achieve your goal. You may work to deepen
   your intuition and to create more positive beliefs.
   Describe in detail your plan for inner work.

_____

_____

_____

5. What are your greatest strengths? Describe them.
   Then focus on the strengths you have, not your
   weaknesses.

_____

_____

_____

Using Synchronicity in 2013

The Swiss psychologist Carl Jung coined the term. It
means the coming together of inner and outer events

in a way that can't be explained by cause and effect and that is meaningful to the observer. Or, it's a meaningful coincidence. When it happens to you, don't dismiss it as a random curiosity. A synchronicity can be a navigational tool, a confirmation, warning, or guidance.

For Frank Morgan, an actor who played five different parts in *The Wizard of Oz*, a stunning synchronicity served as confirmation that he was on the right professional track by accepting parts in the movie.

One of the parts he played was the disreputable Professor Marvel. For that role the director and wardrobe man wanted him dressed in a "nice-looking coat, but tattered," said Mary Mayer, a unit publicist on the film. So they traipsed down to a second-hand clothing store and purchased a rack of coats. Then Frank, the director, and the wardrobe guy all got together and selected one of the coats.

Imagine his surprise when he turned a pocket of the coat inside out and found a name sewn into the lining: L. Frank Baum, the author of *The Wizard of Oz*. The additional synchronicity here is that both men who wore the coat were named Frank.

One of the most common types of synchronicities involves clusters of numbers, names, objects, words, songs, events. Jung experienced many kinds of clusters throughout this life. He believed that numbers are "an archetype of order which has become conscious." So if you begin to experience clusters while you're reinventing your professional life, pay close attention. If the cluster involves a name or the title of a book or song, then it may hold a vital clue about the direction you're taking professionally. If the cluster involves a number, then research its esoteric meaning.

In the past few years hundreds of thousands of people have begun experiencing clusters of 11, 111, and 11:11. Famed Israeli psychic Uri Geller devotes an extensive section of his Web site to 11:11. Several books have been written about it. If you Google 11:11, nearly 200 million links come up. Some of the esoteric meanings: you're on the right track, in the right place at the right time, are being ushered into a greater awareness. So if you begin to notice this particular cluster in your life, know you're headed in exactly the right direction!

While writing this section, we took a break to check the counter on our blog for today and laughed! It was 111.

In times of stress or major transitions—marriage, divorce, birth, a move, career change, or change in employment and income—synchronicities may occur more frequently. Decipher the message if you can, and know that synchronicities indicate we're in the flow, exactly where we're supposed to be.

Your Career Path in 2013

Regardless of what you do for a living, whether you love or detest it or merely tolerate it, you can maximize your strengths and talents to enhance your professional opportunities.

Aries

Ah, Aries. You're restless and impatient. Nothing happens quickly enough for you. As a cardinal fire sign this is to be expected. Your entire life is about movement, action, doing. You're the pioneer, the entrepreneur, the one who really does march to the beat of a different drummer. Your pioneering spirit is your most valuable asset for navigating any professional changes you encounter this year.

Whenever you encounter a challenge or block, you just slam your way through it, leaving a trail of debris in your wake. It might be to your advantage to assess the situation first, then find a gentler means of moving through the block. Usually the word *defeat* doesn't exist in your vocabulary. What someone else might see as a setback, you view as an opportunity.

In 2011 you learned to follow your passions, wherever they led; in 2012 that faith began to pay off; in 2013 the transformation in your professional life should be underway.

Taurus

Few signs are as sensuous and grounded as you are, Taurus. As a fixed earth sign you know your own mind and what you want. Your senses are finely attuned to your environment, you hear the music of the spheres, poetry flows through your dreams, you have the heart and soul of a mystic. You're the most enduring, taciturn, and physical of the twelve signs. You always finish what you start unless it's just unbearable!

In 2011 you learned that your resolute determination is your greatest asset for navigating professional changes. In 2012 you learned to trust your intuition. In 2013 your hard work begins to pay off. Until June 25 of this year expansive Jupiter will be in your financial area, so that's where the payoff begins. Your income should soar. Whether this increase comes from a traditional nine-to-five job or from your own business is irrelevant as long as you're enjoying what you do.

You already know your own value. In 2012 the people around you learned it, and in 2013 they are fully in your court.

Gemini

Your curiosity and ability to communicate with just about anyone anywhere are your greatest assets in 2013. As a mutable air sign flexibility and adapting to change are a snap for you. Your mind is such a hive of activity, buzzing constantly with information, that you just have to get it out somehow, some way. So perhaps 2013 is your time to start a blog or build a Web site, and figure out how to make money from it.

Do you have a particular service to sell? An area of expertise? Have you always wanted to write a book or screenplay? Then as the saying goes, Gemini, there's no time like the present. With 2013 as the year of transformation, it's your turn to shine. In fact until June 25 expansive Jupiter will be in your sign. So plant your seeds during this time, Gemini. Take chances. Expand your horizons. In 2011 you learned to follow the impulses of your curiosity to see where they might lead, and they led some mighty strange places. But you were in the right place at the right time. In 2012 your versatility and communication abilities enabled you to navigate the paradigm shift that's underway. In 2013 you're able to put everything you've learned into action.

Cancer

You're completely attuned to emotions—yours and everyone else's. It's easy for you to slip into someone else's skin and feel what they feel. You hurt as they hurt. You weep as they weep. You laugh as they laugh. Like fellow water sign Pisces you're a psychic sponge, an empath. Your extraordinary memory is intimately linked to your emotions, and your intuition is remarkable. All of these traits helped you to successfully navigate the transitions of 2011. During the first six months of 2012, when Jupiter was in compatible earth sign Taurus, your hard work really began to pay off. You met people who not only shared your interests but who were helpful in some way professionally. Your professional options expanded. Perhaps you launched a business, wrote a novel, had a photography exhibit. One way or another you began to achieve your dreams.

In 2013 you have opportunities to use what you've learned these last two years and put your prodigious intuition to work for you. The period to watch for: June 25, 2013, to mid-July 2014.

Leo

You were born to express your creativity through performance. You love the applause, the recognition, the immediate gratification and feedback. Of course, not every Leo is an actor or actress, but every Leo loves drama. So whether you're on the stage, in front of a classroom, or counseling a patient in therapy, your creative flair moves through you like a force of nature.

In 2011 you learned how valuable this asset was in

helping you to navigate any professional changes you experienced. In 2012 you were well positioned for the unfolding of your dreams. Between January 1 and June 25, 2013, when Jupiter is in compatible air sign Gemini, everything expands for you—opportunity, finances, your personal relationships, your career.

Virgo

Your gift is details. Whether it's your own life that you're honing, sculpting, and shining like some fine gem or a particular project or relationship, you can see the finished product in a way that others can't. You also have a particular gift or ability that you're always willing to provide to others, without thought of compensation. These traits carried you through professional changes you may have experienced in 2011.

The first six months of 2012, when Jupiter was in fellow earth sign Taurus, were probably magnificent for you. Your worldview expanded, you may have traveled extensively overseas, or perhaps a publishing opportunity presented itself. But in 2013, when Jupiter transits your career area, you learn the meaning of professional bliss! The time frame to anticipate: January 1 to June 25, 2013. Prepare yourself for a wild, wonderful career ride.

Libra

You can work a room like a seasoned politician, spreading peace and harmony even among people who can't agree on anything. That's your magic. Yet the very qualities that you can instill in others often elude you. Not that any of us could tell by looking at you. Libra is a master of social camouflage. It seems that nothing ruffles you. But within you're struggling to maintain harmony without compromising your principles. Your sphere is relationships. More than any other sign, you can see the many sides of an issue and understand that your truth may not be everyone's truth. But you can live with the paradox. It's your gift.

Any professional challenges you encountered in 2011 were undoubtedly overcome by your ability to connect with people. In 2012 your professional opportunities proliferated, with enhanced creativity and new travel opportunities tossed in for good measure. In 2013 you're positioned to put it all into action.

Scorpio

You're the emotional vortex of the zodiac, a spinning whirlwind of contradictions. You aren't like the rest of us, and that's the way you prefer it. You dig deeply into everything you do, looking for the absolute bottom line, the most fundamental truth, and then you excavate everything at the discovery site just to make sure you've gotten it all.

Professional challenges that you encountered in 2011 were met with the fortitude and resilience for which you're known. In 2012 you may have launched a business or creative endeavor. In 2013, particularly between June 25, 2013, and mid-July 2014, you may find yourself traveling internationally for business, writing a book or novel, or perhaps heading off for graduate school. Your intuition is finely honed for this period; listen to it.

Sagittarius

You're the life of the party, just like your fellow fire sign Leo. But your approaches are different. Where Leo seeks recognition and applause, you're after the big picture. It doesn't matter how far you have to travel to find it, how many people you have to talk to, how many books or blogs you must read. When your passion is seized, you're as doggedly relentless as Taurus. One part of you operates from raw instinct; the other part is acculturated, aware of how to work the system.

In 2011, the year of transition, you realized that you don't recognize professional challenges. You learned that any bump in a road simply means you take an alternate path to get to where you want to go. In 2012 you may have teamed up with a partner for some entrepreneurial venture or perhaps to launch a business. In 2013 everything comes together in just the way you envisioned. But you may be tempted to take on too much responsibility, so be sure to make specific goals and proceed at a measured, realistic pace.

Capricorn

You're the achiever, the builder, the classic type-A personality whose focus is so tight that everything and everyone becomes part of your journey toward ... well, the top of the hill, the pinnacle of whatever you're attempting to reach. You can build anything, anywhere. A fictional world, belief system, invention, concept, family, video world. Name it, and you can build it.

Any professional challenges you encountered in 2011 were undoubtedly tackled the same way that you have tackled any other challenge in your life—by finding a way around it. Or through it. As a cardinal earth sign you value what is tangible, practical, and efficient, and your journey through any obstacle reflects it. In 2011 you learned how not to fear, and that got you through every professional challenge you encountered. In 2012, when Jupiter was in fellow earth sign Taurus, your muse was so up close and personal that your creativity soared. In 2013, particularly between June 25, 2013, and mid-July 2014, build strong professional partnerships. Learn to delegate.

Aquarius

You're not easy to pigeonhole. Sometimes you seem to be the paragon of independence. Yet you enjoy the company of groups who share your passions. You're the one who thinks so far outside the box that people close to you may accuse you of communication with aliens, ghosts, goblins, elves. Even if it's true, you just laugh and continue on your journey into the strange, the unknown, the heart of the universe.

Any challenges you encountered professionally in 2011 were no major thing for you. You always managed to work your way around the challenge by continuing to explore what interests you. In 2012 your creativity soared and became your most valuable asset for navigating the paradigm shift. In 2013, particularly between January 1 and June 25, when Jupiter is in fellow air sign Gemini, you're on a roll, Aquarius. Whatever you can imagine will manifest itself.

Pisces

Dreamer, healer, mystic: all these adjectives fit you, Pisces. You live within a rich, inner world that is both a buffer and a conduit to deeper experiences. You don't need anyone else to tell you this. At some level you already know it, appreciate it, embrace it. While it's true that you're a sucker for a sob story, an attribute that can turn you from hero to martyr in the space of a single breath, there's no concrete evidence that you're more of a victim than any other sun sign.

Any professional challenges that came your way during 2011 were met with your powerful intuition, prodigious imagination, and unique way of dealing with adversity through faith in your role in the larger scheme of things. The tentacles of your psychic abilities were active 24/7, at your disposal, and awaited your instructions. In 2012 you used your communication abilities to pull ahead of the competition. In 2013 your imagination and intuitive ability get you exactly where you want to be. The time frame to anticipate: June 25, 2013, to mid-July 2014.

CHAPTER 7

Aspects

In astrology we look at where transiting planets fall in the houses of our natal chart and what angles these transiting planets make to our natal planets. These angles are called aspects. For the purpose of this book we primarily look at where these transiting planets hit your solar houses and the angles they make to your sun and to each other. Some of these angles are beneficial, others are challenging.

Think of aspects as a symbolic network of arteries and veins that transport the blood of astrology. In a natal chart these angles connect our inner and outer worlds, accentuate certain traits and play down others. Each aspect represents a certain type of energy, so there really aren't any good or bad aspects because energy is neutral. It's what we do with the energy that counts. It comes back to free will. When transiting planets make angles to each other, energy is also exchanged.

For instance, every year there is at least one very lucky day when the transiting sun and transiting Jupiter form a beneficial angle to each other—a conjunction (same sign and degree), a sextile (60 degrees apart), or a trine (120 degrees apart). The lucky day in 2013 falls on June 18–19, when the sun and Jupiter are within a degree of each other or exactly conjunct. This means that the sun's life energy and Jupiter's expansive energy combine and create, well, some magic for all of us! It's especially good for Taurus and other earth signs, but since we all have Taurus somewhere in our charts, everyone benefits.

If you look back to the presidential election in November 2008, Saturn in Virgo and Uranus in Pisces formed an exact opposition to each other. They were 180 degrees apart, an aspect that is like a tug-of-war. In this case the tug-of-war was between the candidate that represented the old paradigm, the established order — Saturn — and the candidate who symbolized sweeping change — Uranus.

Aspects are most powerful as they are approaching exactness. So even though a conjunction, for example, is 00 degrees of separation or a square is technically 90 degrees of separation, many astrologers use *orbs* that can be as wide as 5 or 10 degrees. Some astrologers use small orbs, but others assign larger orbs for the sun and moon and smaller orbs for other planets. The closer the orb, the more powerful the combination. If you're sensitive to transits, then, you may be feeling lucky for several days before and after June 18–19.

In terms of a natal chart, any transiting planet that is approaching an aspect with one of your natal planets is also most powerful on its approach. The traditional aspects have been used since the second century A.D. They are the conjunction, sextile, square, trine, and opposition. These aspects are considered to be the major or hard angles and are also the most power-ful. There are other minor aspects that astrologers use, but for the purpose of this chapter, we'll only talk about the traditional aspects.

At the end of this chapter is a chart for a young man. We'll be referring to this chart as we discuss the aspects.

Conjunction, major hard aspect, 0 degrees

This aspect is easy to identify—clusters of planets within a few degrees of each other, usually but not always in the same sign and house. But it's a complex aspect because energies combine, fuse, merge. Think of it as power and intensity, and that's true whether it's in your natal chart or is a transiting planet conjuncting your sun sign. If you have conjunctions in your natal chart, the astrologer who reads for you should address what it means and how you can use it to maximize your potential.

Take a look at the young man's chart at the end of the chapter. His fourth and fifth houses are jammed with planets, with just one planet—Mercury—in his third house and just the moon and the South Node in the sixth house. His focus in this lifetime is on creativity and his domestic life. With Uranus, Mars, and Neptune (♅,♂,♆) all in the fifth house, in Sagittarius, this young man's creative interests may involve television or radio (ruled by Uranus). He will pour plenty of energy into his creativity (Mars) and will draw on the resources of his higher self (Neptune) to achieve his creative goals. His Mars and Neptune are exactly conjunct—both at 24 degrees. This aspect is exceptionally powerful, and in self-aware people it unites physical and spiritual energy. He won't have any trouble manifesting his desires and will always attract the people and situations he needs, when he needs them.

Now look at his fourth house. Saturn, Pluto, Venus, the sun, and Jupiter are all crowded in there, with three planets in Libra and two in Scorpio. These planets suggest that his early childhood provided him with a solid foundation from which to live. There may have been some financial deprivation in his early life or excessive rules (Saturn ♄), but there was also enormous power in his family unit that enabled him to discover what made him feel secure and empowered. Venus in Libra suggests that he finds/found great pleasure in his early childhood family life and later as an adult.

With Saturn closely conjunct to both Pluto and Venus, his ambitions find concrete expression through hard work and patience. Romantic relationships are serious business for him. Once his heart is won, his loyalty is unwavering.

Sextile, major soft aspect, 60 degrees

Again, look at the young man's chart. An example of a sextile occurs between his Saturn in Libra at 25 degrees and his Mars and Neptune at 24 degrees Sagittarius. A sextile is a point of ease. It represents a free-flowing energy between the planets involved. No tension. The sextile is a kind of buffer, a shield against turmoil, indecision, instability. But if there are too many sextiles, then the person may be too passive! Again, this definition applies to sextiles within a natal chart as well as transiting sextiles to your sun sign.

The Saturn/Mars sextile suggests that he's a relentless worker, particularly when it comes to the pursuit of his wishes and dreams. He's able to channel his creative drive to achieve whatever he wants. The Saturn/Neptune sextile suggests that the dreamy, spiritual aspects of Neptune are brought down to earth. He believes that every species lives to realize its fullest potential.

There's a 3 degree sextile between Pluto and Venus in Libra and Mars and Neptune in Sagittarius. The Venus/Mars sextile indicates that he gets along well with the opposite sex. His romantic relationships are generally harmonious. Again, the creative aspect in his chart is emphasized. The Pluto/Mars sextile indicates a powerful will and determination. In self-aware individuals there's great metaphysical knowledge and wisdom that can be used to benefit humanity.

Square, major hard aspect, 90 degrees

Friction, angst, *oh my God, the sky is falling*: that's how squares feel in a natal chart. The sky, of course, is never falling, but the friction and angst are quite real and act as triggers for action, forward thrust. They force us to develop, evolve, and reach aggressively for our desires.

In the young man's chart his Capricorn moon in the sixth house (☽♑21) is square to his Saturn in the fourth house (♄♎25). This aspect can be difficult. In fact, many astrologers view it unfavorably. But famed astrologer Grant Lewi called it "the most powerful single aspect you can have in a horoscope. It gives both ambition and the ability to concentrate on it."

This young man, by the way, is now a successful videographer and filmmaker, a business he has built from the bottom up, on his own hard work and focus.

His Mercury in the third house ($\text{☿}\triangle14$) forms a wide square to his Capricorn moon. Generally this square indicates a conflict between head and heart. His emotions tell him one thing, his head screams another. It's likely that the young man has a magnetic wit, can talk to anyone about anything, and has a great sense of humor.

Trines, major soft aspect, 120 degrees

This aspect works like a sextile, linking energies in a harmonious way. It's associated with general ease and good fortune, and it's the same whether it's in the natal chart or by transit.

Look at the chart again. The only trine this young man has occurs between his Mars in Sagittarius and his Midheaven—the cusp of his tenth house. This trine enables him to achieve whatever he desires professionally, and he's willing to work hard for it. He may travel internationally too, in some professional capacity. Mars rules Aries, so it rules his Midheaven—a major plus.

Opposition, major hard aspect, 180 degrees

This aspect feels like a persistent itch that you can't reach and usually involves polarities—Taurus/Scorpio, for example, or Aries/Libra. It brings about change through conflict and sometimes represents traits we project onto others because we haven't fully integrated them into ourselves. Again, the opposition applies to transits as well as to natal planets.

Due to the way the planets are clumped in this man's chart, the only opposition he has is between Mercury in Libra and his Midheaven in Aries. This man will be happiest and most productive when he's self-employed. His ideas might conflict with those of any boss. His ingenuity is abundant, and one way or another he gets his ideas across.

When planets transit this man's empty houses, particularly the houses that are directly opposite those in which the majority of his natal planets fall, he's apt to feel it strongly. This year, for instance, Uranus in Aries will be approaching an opposition with his natal Mercury. But because of Uranus' retrograde motion, the opposition won't be exact until 2014. During its approach to that exactness his daily life will pick up speed, new and exciting opportunities will infuse his awareness, and he may travel abroad on the spur of the moment. His communication abilities will be razor sharp. He may feel restless, have many brilliant and cutting edge ideas, and could be casting around for a way to express all of it.

In late summer 2015 Uranus will be approaching its opposition to his natal Saturn, Pluto, and Venus, which are all in the late degrees of Libra. Since Uranus takes seven years to transit a sign, these oppositions won't be exact until late spring and early summer of 2017.

Some other minor aspects that astrologers use are:

- the semi-square, 45 degrees. It creates irritation and friction between the planets involved.
- the septile, 51 degrees. Indicative of harmony and union in a nontraditional way. Can suggest spiritual power.
- the quincunx or inconjunct, 150 degrees separation. Indicates a need for adjustment in attitude and beliefs.

EXAMPLE CHART 2013

Oct 24, 1982
00:22:00 AM EDT
EXAMPLE CHART 2013
Asheville, NC
ZONE: +04:00
082W33'15"
35N36'03"

Geocentric
Tropical
Koch Houses

Sunday Oct 24, 1982
The 297th day of this year.
00:22:00 AM EDT +04:00
LMT: 22.51.47*
UT: 04.22.00
UT-LMT: 05:30.13
ST   01h00m47s
RAMC: 019°12'
Local Apparent Time: 23.07:31
Equation of Time: 15m44s
Planetary Hour Sun (☉)
6th Hour of Saturn-Night
Sunrise (approx.) 07 48 EDT
Sunset (approx.) 18:41 EDT
Moon in 1st Quarter
☉/☽ Angle   081°05'
☽'s Motion: +11°47'46"

| 0 | 0 |
| 1 | 9 |

Adjusted Calculation Dates
0h: Aug 18   12h: Feb 17

CHAPTER 8

Moon Days

Collective Concepts of the Moon

Throughout the millennia, the moon has been the stuff of myths and fairy tales, poetry and legends. It has been worshipped and cursed and endowed with magical and curative powers. Religions have grown up around it. Sacrifices have been made to it.

In the early fifties the moon was a favorite theme in science fiction books and movies, and the storylines rarely varied: the aliens came from the moon, we colonized the moon, or the moon fell out of orbit . . . you get the general picture. Even Disney issued movies in which the moon played a vital role. In one film, a Western, a woman who wore a hoop skirt typical of the American west started bouncing and kept bouncing higher and higher until she bounced right into the moon. The shadow you see in the moon is, according to Disney, that woman in the hoop skirt.

In 1969 Neil Armstrong took one giant step for mankind, and our concept of the moon was forever changed. Even though its relative position in the sky hadn't changed, everything else about it had.

We now had some idea what it really looked like, and the news was far from good. Dust, dust, and more dust. A black vacuum. Unimaginable cold. Nothingness. What's most vivid in our minds, though, is how the Earth looked from the moon—a swirling turquoise gem, a blue pearl turning in space. Our planet literally looked alive.

This was the year when Vietnam was in full swing. Americans arrived home in body bags, riots swept across college campuses, LSD was the drug of choice. People were tuning in and dropping out faster than the pictures of the moon were beamed back to Earth.

This was the year that half a million people converged on the tiny town of Woodstock, New York, to hear Hendrix, Baez, Dylan, Joplin, and all the other musicians who had captured the emotional reality of war and chaos. Women threw off their shackles. Carlos Castaneda and Aldous Huxley hurled open the doors to other realities. Camelot was dead, Martin Luther King was dead, and we had walked on the moon.

In many ways those steps of Armstrong's signaled that we were ready to confront our unconscious selves, our feminine, intuitive selves.

Fast-forward to the summer of 1997, July 4 to be exact. In the opening scenes of the movie *Independence Day*, a mammoth shadow falls across the surface of the moon. A moving shadow whose shape is unmistakable. The message comes through loud and clear: the shadow is that of a spaceship that uses the moon as a base, and now that ship is on the move toward Earth. What ensues is pure Hollywood, with Will Smith holding the record for aliens annihilated. But *Independence Day*, like Armstrong's giant step, is part of our contemporary collective perception of the moon, its essential beauty and sublime mysteries.

Despite Hollywood and NASA, each of us has some personal concept about the moon. After all, we drop our heads back on any given night and there it is, shaped like a ubiquitous eye or the grin of a Cheshire cat or like a piece of fruit with the top lopped off. It speaks to us. We speak to it. Romance, madness, werewolves, witches, pagans, Druids, ocean tides and blood tides, or a sharp rise in murder and mayhem; it's all fair game where the moon is concerned. Every notion that we hold about the moon is true *for us,* and that subjective texture is certainly in keeping with the nature of the moon in astrology.

If the sun is where you shine in your corner of the universe, then the moon is your personal oracle. If the sun represents your life force, then the moon represents the internal landscape that supports and maintains the life force. In astrology, lunar energy is embodied in that mythological moment when Luke Skywalker recognizes that Darth Vader is his father or when in *ET* the alien is getting drunk and the boy is trying to dissect a frog at school and their psyches mesh. Lunar energy is operating when reality splits off for the character Gywneth Paltrow plays in *Sliding Doors* or during the love scene in *Titanic*.

Lunar energy is the MO in *Thelma and Louise, Jacob's Ladder,* and *What Dreams May Come.* It's the psychic visions the young boy has in *The Shining* or the visions another young boy has in *The Sixth Sense*.

It's the mother's anguish in *The Deep End of the Ocean,* and it used to be Oprah being Oprah weekday afternoons. Without lunar energy, we would be empty shells, automatons, the burn-the-books society in *Fahrenheit 451.* We would be Keanu Reeves still stuck in the matrix, powerless puppets who accept everything at face value.

Lunar Facts and Oddities

Most of us learn facts about the moon in grade-school science class. Today's kids have a distinct advantage over their parents, of course, because we've already been to the moon, and information is so readily accessible through the Internet.

The moon is our only satellite, and its average distance from Earth is 238,857 miles. Its revolution around the Earth takes 27 days, seven hours, and 43 minutes. Even though it's only a quarter the size of Earth, its gravitational pull is the main cause of our ocean tides. In fact the moon actually has more than twice the effect on tides as the sun.

Since our bodies are primarily water, the moon's gravitational pull on the tides also affects our bodily fluids, metabolic rates, and, of course, our emotions. The link, for instance, between the full moon and violent aggression has been noted for years by police officers, hospital workers, and employees at mental institutions.

In the 1970s a Miami psychiatrist, Arnold Lieber, decided to conduct a scientific study to find out if these observations were true. As a med student at

Jackson Memorial Hospital in Miami, he'd noticed recurring periods when patients on the psyche ward were more disturbed than usual. These periods would last for several days, then the patients would resume their normal behavior. He became curious about the phenomenon and finally conducted a scientific study. His findings, later backed by four other independent studies, confirmed that during the full moon and, to a lesser extent, during the new moon there are increases in all violent crimes—homicide, rape, assault. There's also an increase in lesser crimes—burglary, auto theft, larceny, and drunken and disorderly behavior.

Is it any coincidence, then, that the word *lunatic* is derived from the word *lunar*?

Hospital workers and maternity ward nurses have long noticed that more babies are born at the full and new moons than at any other time of the month. These may be due to the fact that the gravitational pull is strongest when the moon, sun, and Earth are aligned, as they are during the new and full moon. These observations have been backed by scientific studies. Interestingly enough, the lunar calendar is still the basis for calculating a pregnancy. The nine months are synodic months (the length of time it takes the moon to orbit Earth).

Since the moon has no atmosphere, it has nothing to protect it from meteor strikes, which is why its surface is pocked with impact craters. Since it has no tectonic or volcanic activity, its surface is immune to the erosive effects of atmospheric weathering, tectonic shifts, and volcanic upheavals that reshape the surface of our planet. In comparison Earth is a work in progress. On the moon even the footprints left by the

Apollo astronauts will remain intact for millions of years unless a meteor strike obliterates them.

The moon's gravity is about a sixth of ours; that's why the Apollo astronauts looked like they were jumping rope up there. Despite appearances to the contrary, the moon has no light of its own. That gorgeous full moon you see each month is the reflected light of our sun.

In ancient cultures the passage of time was marked according to the lunation—or cycle—of the moon. A *month* was the time between one new moon and the next, and in a typical year there were thirteen lunar cycles. This way of marking time still exists among some pagan sects, and may be closer to our natural rhythms than our present solar calendar.

Astrological Lunar Facts

The moon in your horoscope is every bit as important as your sun sign. In fact, Eastern astrologers give the moon greater emphasis than the sun sign. The moon rules the sign of Cancer and the fourth house in the horoscope. She represents mom or whoever plays that role for you and also symbolizes other women in your life. The moon is feminine, yin, our intuitive selves.

In the physical body her territory pertains primarily to women—breasts, ovaries, womb. In both genders she rules internal fluids and the stomach, and of course she's our emotional barometer, the gauge of our inner health. Not surprisingly, the moon rules conception.

A Czech physician, in fact, theorized that every

woman had a fertility cycle that depended on the phase of the moon when she was born. Eugene Jones developed a fertilization calendar based on his theory, which allegedly showed a 98 percent success rate. He charged an astronomical fee for his calendar, but people who were desperate for children paid it.

Jones claimed that if a woman used his methods, she could choose the gender of her child. His technique was based on the rules of classical astrology, which he'd studied, and boils down to using the gender of moon signs. If conception took place on a Leo day, the child would be male. On a Taurus day the child would be a girl.

The medical establishment went berserk over his claims. But when a panel of gynecologists challenged him to predict the genders of babies based only on their conception dates, Jones' accuracy was 87 percent.

If you don't know the sign of your natal moon, check any of the astrology sites listed in this book and get a free birth chart. You'll need your exact time of birth, place, and of course the date!

The Transiting Moon

The moon changes signs every two and a half days. As you follow along in the daily prediction section for your sign, you'll be able to keep tabs on where the moon is on any given day. Certain activities are favored on certain lunar days, so let's take a look at how you can maximize the transiting moon's energy in your life.

Aries Moon

Cardinal fire sign

This is the day to be a fearless entrepreneur, to move forward on projects that have been sitting on the back burner for weeks or months. It's a great time to initiate new projects too, especially those that have been rattling around in the back of your head for some time.

You may feel restless and impatient with others, so the best way to deal with it is to pour that energy into something about which you feel passionate. Others see you as a leader, as the person with answers. You attract individuals who are eager to be on your team. You feel more self-sufficient, capable of doing whatever needs to be done.

Follow your impulses regardless of how odd they may seem. Sometimes our impulses are the universe's way of leading us toward a new opportunity, a new relationship, a new creative project. Since Mars rules Aries, physical activity is heightened. Take a yoga class. Join the gym. Go walking. Weather permitting, it's a great day for a hike, a bike ride, a long swim.

It's a good day to *believe* that whatever you desire can manifest itself. Your intentions and focus are key.

Taurus Moon

Fixed earth sign

The moon loves Taurus as much as it loves Cancer, the sign that it rules. In Taurus lunar energies work effortlessly, smoothly, and that makes your intuition easier to develop and use.

On a Taurus moon day think about that children's story *Ferdinand the Bull*. The author probably wasn't thinking about Taurus when he created the character, but Ferdinand is the perfect archetype for Taurus. Ferdinand enjoyed peaceful surroundings, and today so do you. In fact, peacefulness and harmony are vital to your emotional well-being. You need these qualities the way a Gemini moon needs books or education or communication with other people.

It will take a lot to anger you today, but repeated provocation can trigger your "bull's rush" fury, the human equivalent of Ferdinand's reaction to the bee sting. Some of the things that can set you off are: incessant nagging by someone who wants you to do something you don't want to do; insistence that you act in a particular way; unreasonable demands or actions by anyone.

A Taurus moon day enables you to stick with something right to the end. You won't be a quitter. You will also be slow to change your mind and opinion and won't be rushed or cajoled into doing something that doesn't interest you.

If you enjoy gardening or have a particular artistic passion, then today is the day to indulge!

Gemini Moon

Mutable air sign

Today your nemesis is boredom. Its possibility unnerves you. If you were put in a bare room without windows, books, TV, radio, computer, paper, pen, phone, fax, or anything else, you would freak within the hour. This may be true of the other air-sign moons as well, but for the Gemini moon it's a sure thing. Your emotional well-being needs mental stimulation and the means to communicate with others.

It's a good day to start blogging, if you haven't already, to dust off that old manuscript you were working on way back when, or to get together with friends and shoot the breeze. You may feel compelled to sign up for a workshop or even an online course in something that interests you. Or you may decide to go to college or graduate school. It's a great day for research, for delving into a topic or concern and finding out everything you can about it.

Communication, whatever form it takes, is paramount.

Cancer Moon

Cardinal water sign

Today your memories work overtime. You're able to conjure sights, smells, tastes, sounds, and textures from your past in vivid detail. The event you're recalling may have happened thirty years ago, but in your memory it's just as fresh and detailed as the day it occurred.

The moon rules Cancer, so it's at home in this sign. This is where its energies express themselves most smoothly. Today your emotions are racing through you, and it may be easy to have your feelings hurt. Your acute sensitivity makes you feel vulnerable, and it isn't easy for you to step back and view a situation or relationship dispassionately.

Family, home, and roots are especially important to you today. Schedule time to be with the people you love. Whether it's a traditional family or friends whom you love like family, you draw comfort and sustenance from these individuals. It's a good time to work on creative projects; your inspiration comes from deep places within you. During the Cancer moon you may have a real soft spot for animals—strays that drop by your place for a bowl of food, the neighbor's cat that sneaks into your house. A visit to your local pound may be in order!

Leo Moon

Fixed fire sign

It's a perfect day to showcase your talents. In fact, when you enter a room, people notice you. If for some reason they don't, then you make sure that they do. This isn't just an ego thing, either. Applause and being noticed are vital to your well-being today even if your only audience is your family. *You need to be recognized as someone special.*

Your flair for drama today is remarkable. It runs through everything you do—from the way you dress, speak, and act to the activities in which you engage. You may decide to take in a play or try out for a part. Creatively, you're at the top of your game, and anything you undertake will bear this dramatic stamp.

It's a good day to spend time with your kids doing something everyone enjoys, to volunteer at an animal shelter, get out and be seen, socialize, make new contacts. Network. Be as flamboyant as you can imagine.

Virgo Moon

Mutable earth sign

Today you're on a quest for perfection and the words *Be the best that you can* take on a whole new dimension of meaning. You thrive on order and manage to use today's lunar energy to tackle emotional chaos in your life and impose order on it.

Virgo tends to be a health-oriented sign, so today favors starting a new diet, nutritional program, exercise regimen. Even if you're already involved in these areas, consider fine-tuning the details. You also may want to consider blogging or writing about what you're learning about health, nutrition, exercise.

Today also favors performing a service for someone else—not for pay, not with any thought of compensation, but as a good deed. This could mean anything from volunteering at your favorite charity to putting in some time at an animal rescue sanctuary. Pay attention to your spiritual beliefs today. Are you in tune with a greater good? Are your thoughts the most positive they can be?

Libra Moon

Cardinal air sign

Among astrologers certain moon signs stir the soul for the sheer beauty of what they represent. The Taurus moon is one of these. The Libra moon is another.

Today, at the heart of it, you're a lover, a true romantic. Moonlit beaches, bouquets of roses, books of poetry, going to the opera, a summer rain: this is the language your soul speaks during the Libra moon. So first of all surround yourself with beauty today—music, scenery, people. Just the sight of all this beauty will deepen your appreciation for life.

It's a good day for group work—in your community or with your students, peers, fellow workers. Or it's a great time to socialize and network. Today your interests tend toward people and relationships, your artistic interests, and attaining peace and harmony. You can see both sides of an issue with greater clarity and try to avoid conflict.

The Libra moon can enhance your intuition, so try to follow your hunches today and see where they lead you. If you don't meditate yet, today is a terrific time to start. It doesn't have to be lengthy. In fact, five minutes in a quiet place with your mind still is all you need. You'll come out of it refreshed. Keep track of any impressions that come your way during those five minutes.

If you're in a committed relationship, then be sure to spend time with your partner. Have a romantic dinner at home or at your favorite restaurant. Talk and get in touch with each other.

Scorpio Moon

Fixed water sign

Emotionally, it's a powerful day. You feel everything so intensely that it's as if some new, inner part of you has awakened from a deep sleep. You may feel as if you've been seized by a force beyond your control. Despite how it feels, this sense of outside forces is just an illusion. Your emotions are your most powerful allies today. They provide you with a direct, immediate connection to the deepest parts of your intuitive self and are capable of instantly transforming your reality.

This transformation happens when you bring your considerable will, intent, and desire to bear against whatever it is that you want to change. When the energy of this moon is focused and backed with passion, this change occurs at the quantum level and can result in the remission of illness or disease, sudden rise in wealth and fame, an explosion of psychic ability ... well, you get the general idea.

Scorpio is also about power—the power we wield over others and the power others wield over us. All too often this lunar energy is misused or abused when it concerns power issues; then its tremendous capacity for positive transformation becomes negative. The difference seems to be self-awareness.

It's a great day to work with healing energies, intuitive and psychic development, and research and investigation.

Sagittarius Moon

Mutable fire sign

Oh, baby, let the good times roll! For the Sagittarian moon, those good times mean music, deep talk, exotic travel, esoteric ideas. Today you're an explorer. Those explorations may take you to the farther ends of the Earth or deep within the mysteries of the universe. In one way or another this moon enables you to search for the higher truth, the larger picture, a more expansive perspective.

You may be more blunt than usual when dealing with people today, particularly when the other guy just doesn't get what seems so obvious to you. Patience and nuance aren't your strong points during this period. The exception to this occurs when you're pursuing something about which you feel passionate, then you have the patience of Mother Teresa and are as detail oriented as a Virgo.

You're called to action today. You would rather do than think about doing. As a mutable sign, you're emotionally adaptable. You have opinions about virtually everything and aren't the least bit hesitant in expressing these opinions. This becomes a problem if you're dogmatic or bombastic about what you believe and try to convert others to your way of thinking. So today strive to nurture patience and optimism.

Capricorn Moon

Cardinal earth sign

The moon isn't particularly comfortable in this sign. It chafes at all the rules and restrictions that Capricorn seeks to impose and dislikes all that earthy grounding. However, this moon certainly favors strategy—laying out goals and figuring ways to achieve them. Your physical energy is excellent today and enables you to work long hours to meet a deadline, regardless of whether that deadline is self-imposed (which it often is) or imposed by a boss.

You feel quite independent today and may find yourself outdoors, hiking alone through the wilderness or at the gym, putting in extra time on the treadmill. Under this lunar influence, you push yourself, move the bar higher, and feel a certain determination to carve your niche in the larger world.

Today it's easier to categorize your emotions, to look at things dispassionately. So tackle stuff that pushes your buttons, issues that you've pushed aside but which beg for a resolution.

Aquarius Moon

Fixed air sign

Today you march to a different drummer. You may hear a different kind of music in your very cells and feel compelled to decipher the message and act on it. This is the sign, after all, that ushers in new paradigms by refusing to go along with the status quo.

The visionary component to this moon sign gives you an edge today on new trends. You can spot the next wave long before anyone else does. The trick is acting on it and putting it to work for you in your personal and professional life. Your rational mind may try to intervene, to argue and put up blocks, to keep you within the confining box of consensus reality. Or someone close to you—a parent, close friend, significant other—inadvertently plays that role, and you suddenly find yourself on the defensive.

So today be fearless. Go forward secure in the knowledge that your vision is correct!

Pisces Moon

Mutable water sign

Today you're the archetypal dreamer, your feet never really firmly rooted on the earth. You're deeply compassionate today too, a true bleeding heart. You probably won't be able to pass a homeless person on the street without giving him money, and you definitely won't resist the soulful gaze of a stray pup or kitten. Injustices of any sort may fill you with a deep sadness. Your challenge during this moon is to detach emotionally from situations and people who cause you this kind of anguish.

Part of the problem is that today you're a psychic sponge who soaks up the emotions and moods of the people around you. This alone makes it vital that you associate with upbeat, positive people and situations that boost your energy rather than sap it.

The Pisces moon favors imagination, intuition, any artistic endeavor. On a strictly mundane level it's a fine day to shop for new clothes, get a new hairdo, redesign yourself in some way. Also, your dreams should be especially vivid and could contain important insights and information.

⚖️ CHAPTER 9

Money, Luck, and Synchronicity in 2013

Money and luck don't necessarily go hand in hand. Vast fortunes are often made because the individual had vision and was able to make that vision a concrete reality. Sometimes people are simply in the right place at the right time and play their cards exactly right. Usually synchronicity plays a major role. Let's take a closer look.

The word, coined by Swiss psychiatrist Carl Jung, means the coming together of inner and outer events in a way that is meaningful to the observer and can't be explained by cause and effect. Or: meaningful co-incidence. We've all experienced these events. You're thinking of a friend you haven't seen for years, and suddenly you get an invite from that person on Face-book. Or you're delayed on your way to work one morning, and when you finally arrive at your turnoff discover there was an accident at just about the time you would have driven through if you'd been on time.

Once you're aware that these incidents hold a deeper meaning, they tend to happen more frequently. As you begin to work with these synchronicities, deciphering their messages, you suddenly realize you're in the flow, in the right place at the right time.

The planet that can help us get into the flow—Jupiter—is also the planet that represents luck and expansion, success, prosperity, growth, creativity, spiritual interests, higher education, and the law. It also governs publishing, overseas travel, and foreign countries and our dealings with them. This year it will be in two signs. Between January 1 and June 25, it will be transiting air sign Gemini. Between June 25, 2013, and July 16, 2014, it will be transiting Cancer. Let's take a look at how these transits might attract more synchronicity, luck, and prosperity into your life this year.

Aries

If you aren't aware of synchronicity, then your best time this year for delving into this fascinating phenomenon is between January 1 and June 25, while Jupiter in Gemini moves through your solar third house of communication. You may want to keep a journal about your experiences as the synchros occur and to note what types of synchronicities they are. Do they occur in clusters, with the same name, word, or phrase happening repeatedly during a relatively short period of time? Do your experiences act as guidance, confirmation, warnings?

It's relatively easy for you to get into the flow, Aries. Just follow your impulses. They often lead you to exactly where you need to be. If you have a hunch that you should follow a particular course, by all means follow the hunch. If a dream provides what seems to be information about an issue that concerns you, be sure to consider this information before making a decision. Financially, if you are careful about impulse spending, you should do well during Jupiter's transit of Gemini. Be sure to pay attention to Mercury retrograde periods, however, and avoid buying large-ticket items during those times.

Between June 25, 2013, and July 16, 2014, when Jupiter is in Cancer, you can easily apply what you've learned during the previous six months. Your home life/domestic environment may be expanding in some way, so be sure to watch for synchros in that area. Your intuition will increase, and your hunches should proliferate during this period.

Taurus

Your finances should be expanding during the first six months of the year. In fact, if money is your focus, then it's likely your synchronicities will occur within the financial area. You may discover, for instance, that you have a hunch to buy a particular stock, and when you follow the hunch the stock rises within a day. Later when someone asks why you bought that particular stock, you won't really know why, except that you *had a feeling*.

During Jupiter's transit through Cancer you're going to be in a strong position to talk about your synchronicities, your luck, how your life is expanding. You may want to blog about it, to reach out to other like-minded individuals. Your capacity for communication will expand appreciably during this year-long transit. Your intuition should be exceptionally strong too, particularly as it relates to your neighborhood and community.

Gemini

When Jupiter transits your sign during the first six months of 2013, your life will be expanding in numerous directions. One of those areas will be your finances. Be sure to stay on top of things, Gemini, especially if the money is rolling in faster than you can count it. Check and recheck your bank statements, stocks, investment portfolio, 401K contributions, even pay stubs. Don't be obsessive about it, just take responsibility for where your money goes and how you spend it.

During this transit you won't just *feel* lucky, you'll actually *be* lucky. Your optimism and generally positive outlook on life will attract what you need before you need it. New people and opportunities will enter your life, and you'll have plenty of choices to make. All the stuff that unfolds during the first six months of 2013 prepares you for Jupiter's transit of Cancer and your financial area between June 25, 2013, and July 16, 2014. Initially this transit may bring about some hefty expenditures, but sometimes you have to spend money to make money! By mid-July 2014 your financial affairs will be looking quite grand.

Cancer

During the first half of the year Jupiter transits your solar twelfth house. This period brings heightened insights concerning your own psyche and unconscious. You may try therapy, take up meditation. Jupiter's transit through Gemini makes your unconscious more accessible to you in some way, and you discuss the process with others through a blog or Web site, by writing a book, keeping a journal. You may even work this process into your professional life in some way. One purpose for this transit is to clear out the old to make way for the new when Jupiter enters your sign. You may be discarding beliefs that no longer serve your best interests, breaking longstanding habits. Relationships may end, but new ones begin.

By the time Jupiter enters Cancer on June 25, you're ready for the adventure, whatever it may be. Your financial picture should expand considerably—a plump raise, a new business venture, royalties. Your intuition is greatly enhanced during this transit, and you're able to create a rich psychic environment for synchronicity. Be sure to decipher the messages of these synchros; they hold valuable information for you.

Leo

The first Jupiter transit this year expands your circle of friends, acquaintances, and connections. You're able to network effectively and find the support you need for new projects and ventures. You may experience synchronicities that involve other people. You might, for instance, dream of someone you know you've never met—only to meet that same person the next day or a week later. Any seeds you sow during this transit will be beneficial down the line, Leo. Since the transit occurs in Gemini, consider putting up a Web site or starting a blog on a topic about which you're passionate.

During the second transit, which lasts about a year, you're journeying through your own unconscious, which is more readily accessible to you. It's similar to what Cancer experiences when Jupiter transits its twelfth house, but with an important difference. Cancer enjoys solitude; you generally don't. So for you this transit can best be used by joining a meditation class or taking up yoga or tai chi. In other words, get involved with classes, where you have people around you. Your synchros during this period may involve guidance on issues you must settle before Jupiter enters your sign in mid-2014.

Virgo

The first part of the year focuses on an expansion in your career, Virgo. You might get promoted, land a nice raise, change jobs or careers to something that suits you better. Synchronicities you experience may revolve around career issues and concerns. Be sure to decode the messages that come with these synchros; they could prove helpful as guidance and confirmation. Your precision and attention to detail during this time should aid you if you assume a lot of responsibility, as you're apt to do.

During the second Jupiter transit, which lasts about a year, you'll really be in your element. Friends, acquaintances, and social groups will be lucky for you, and your social circle should expand tremendously. The connections you make will prove to be beneficial and will expand your worldview in some way. Synchronicities, once you're aware of them, should come fast and furiously, and you won't have any trouble deciphering them. Your particular mindset lends itself to solving puzzles and mysteries.

Libra

During the first six months of the year, while Jupiter transits fellow air sign Gemini, your opportunities for expansion should be remarkable. The ninth house governs your worldview, higher education, publishing, and foreign travel, so expansions are likely to take place in those areas. Your communication opportunities should expand as well. You might sell a book or novel you've written, might go to college or graduate school, may sign up for a seminar or workshop on a topic about which you're passionate. If you travel a great deal during this period, don't be surprised if you begin to experience a flurry of synchronicities.

While Jupiter transits Cancer between June 25, 2013, and July 16, 2014, it will be moving through your career area. This period should be exciting, with your professional opportunities multiplying almost more quickly than you can keep up with. You'll be lucky professionally—you're the right person at the right time and place, that sort of lucky. You may change jobs or careers, and if you do, it's for a better position and more pay. You could also be promoted or may decide to launch your own business.

Scorpio

During Jupiter's transit through Gemini and your solar eighth house (until June 25, 2013) your partner's income will expand, and you may be delving more deeply into metaphysics. Your intuitive abilities should deepen considerably under this transit—and you're already one of the most psychic signs in the zodiac! You may be researching and investigating life after death, communication with spirits, haunted houses, things that go bump in the night. You'll be fortunate with mundane things as well—mortgages, loans, taxes, insurance, all of which falls under the eighth house.

Jupiter's transit through fellow water sign Cancer—June 25, 2013, to July 16, 2014—will be very much to your liking, Scorpio. This one should expand your opportunities for foreign travel and broadening your worldview and spiritual beliefs. You may sample different religions or spiritual beliefs, launch a spiritual quest, even travel to far-flung locales in search of spiritual truths. It all depends, Scorpio, on what you're seeking and how sincere you are in your desires.

Sagittarius

Since Jupiter rules your sign, its movements impact you quite personally and powerfully. During the first six months, when Jupiter transits your opposite, Gemini, your partnership opportunities increase. You may find exactly the right business or romantic partner or both. If you're involved in a relationship, then you may decide to deepen your commitment—move in together, get engaged, or marry. Synchronicities you experience are likely to be related to partnerships and issues concerning commitment and communication.

Between June 25, 2013, and July 16, 2014, Jupiter transits Cancer and your solar eighth house. The eighth house dynamics are always intriguing. On one side you have mundane issues—taxes, insurance, bank loans, and mortgages—and on the other side you have esoteric stuff —hauntings, life after death, communication with the dead. These issues will be focal points for expansion. Synchronicities are likely to abound in these areas. It should be easier for you to obtain a mortgage and bank loan, and you will find yourself drawn to explore things that go bump in the night. You may even travel abroad to investigate crop circles or UFO reports. It all depends on how far outside the box your interests extend.

Capricorn

During the first six months of the year, when Jupiter is transiting Gemini and your solar sixth house, your responsibilities at work increase. You may be putting in longer hours, but enjoying your work more. Your communication with coworkers and employees is more frequent and lively, and you find camaraderie with coworkers who think along the same lines that you do.

If you've been unemployed, then this transit should help you land a job that not only pays the bills, but which makes you feel more optimistic generally about your life. Despite what you see around you in terms of financial hardships others may be experiencing, your world feels more secure.

Once Jupiter enters Cancer, your opposite sign (June 25, 2013, to July 16, 2014), your partnership opportunities increase. If you're involved in a relationship already, then you and your partner may move in together, get engaged, or marry. Professional partnerships are also impacted by this transit. Let's say you've started your own business but may be lacking in the financial department until the business gets off the ground. Jupiter in Cancer helps you find the right partner, at the right time.

Synchronicities tend to happen more frequently when we're in transitional phases of our lives, so pay attention to them. They can guide you and act as confirmation for your choices.

Aquarius

While Jupiter is in fellow air sign Gemini, you're in a very good place, Aquarius. The first six months of the year should bring expansion in the areas of romance, creativity, and everything you do for pleasure. If you've thought about starting a family, then Jupiter in Gemini and your solar fifth house could help bring that about. If you weren't involved when this transit began last year, then you probably are now and are thoroughly enjoying yourself. Creatively, you're on a definite roll. Your muse is whispering to you 24/7, and you awaken each morning with a song in your heart, eager to embrace the day.

Between June 25, 2013, and July 16, 2014, Jupiter moves through water sign Cancer and your solar sixth house. This transit brings an expansion in your daily work. You may land a promotion, get a raise, hire new employees for your business, spend more time socializing with coworkers. With Jupiter in the nurturing sign of Cancer, you may experience an expansion in your domestic situation too. Perhaps a parent moves in or a child moves back home after college. You may build an addition to your home.

Synchronicities come in all shapes and forms. Don't

dismiss any meaningful coincidence as just random weirdness. Take a deeper look; decipher the message.

Pisces

Jupiter corules your sign, so its transits are always significant for you. During the first six months, while Jupiter transits Gemini and your solar fourth house, your domestic situation expands in some way. Perhaps your significant other moves in with you. Or you and your partner have a child. Or a parent moves in. Or, equally possible, you may move — across town, across the country, or to another country.

Between June 25, 2013, and July 16, 2014, Jupiter transits fellow water sign Cancer, and you're in the driver's seat, Pisces. This transit bolsters your imagination, creative abilities, and capacity for enjoyment. Love and romance are tops on your list, and you have no shortage of opportunities in these areas. Synchronicities are likely to swirl through your life during this transit, and because you're so innately psychic you get the message easily.

CHAPTER 10

The Thirteenth Sign

On January 10, 2011, the *Minneapolis Star Tribune* carried an article about the emergence of a possible thirteenth zodiac sign. The story apparently zipped around cyberspace at the speed of light and was picked up by CNN, ABC, and NBC. Network coverage on this topic struck me as weird: since when do they cover astrology?

It was covered because an astronomer—not an astrologer—made the announcement about the thirteenth sign and presented a new set of dates for all the signs, shifting the zodiac. Paul Kunkle, who teaches astronomy at a junior college in Minneapolis, pointed out that the zodiac periods were set up by the Babylonians millennia ago. Since then the moon's gravitational pull has made the Earth "wobble" on its axis, which has created a one-month difference in the stars' alignment over time. "When astrologers say the sun is in Pisces, it's really not in Pisces," said Kunkle. "Most horoscope readers who consider themselves Pisces are actually Aquarians."

Here's how the dates line up under Kunkle's theory:

Aries: April 18–May 13
Taurus: May 13–June 21
Gemini: June 21–July 20
Cancer: July 20–August 10
Leo: August 10–September 16
Virgo: September 16–October 30
Libra: October 30–November 23
Scorpio: November 23–November 29
Ophiuchus: November 29–December 17
Sagittarius: December 17–January 20
Capricorn: January 20–February 16
Aquarius: February 16–March 11
Pisces: March 11–April 18

Notice the new sign for November 29 to December 17? That's Ophiuchus (OFF-ee-YOO-kuss), the Serpent Bearer, which in Kunkle's view now belongs in the mainstream zodiac.

However, Kunkle's dates are irrelevant for Western astrology; he's actually referring to sidereal astrology, which is oriented to the constellations. Tropical astrology, the most common form in the Western world, is based on the seasons. It's geocentric—related to life on Earth. In tropical astrology, if you were born between February 19 and March 20, you're still a Pisces!

The irony is that the ancient Babylonians knew about Ophiuchus, but because they didn't want a zodiac with thirteen signs they tossed it out. They supposedly thought that thirteen wasn't as tidy as twelve. It was one of the forty-eight constellations listed by the second-century astronomer Ptolemy and is one of the eighty-eight modern constellations. As you can see, though Ophiuchus may be new to us, it has been around for centuries.

But what should we make of its recent reappearance in the astrological conversation? Perhaps, in a larger context, its rediscovery signals the emergence of a new planetary archetype, and its importance can be found in what it might be telling us about humanity and ourselves at this juncture in time. That's where synchronicity enters the picture.

Planets are archetypes—Mars, for instance, is the mythological god of war; Venus is the mythological goddess of love. A planet's discovery often "coincides" with a shift in mass consciousness that comes about as certain world events and situations unfold. For example, in 1930 a new planet was discovered as a result of aberrations in the orbit of Uranus. The planet was named Pluto, after the god of the underworld. In mythology Pluto is associated with Hades— hell—and with immense power and destruction. In Latin literature Pluto also rules the dead. In astrology this planet came to be associated with profound and irrevocable change, transformation, strange taboos, dictators, decadence, disasters, atomic power, gangsters (Mafia), sexuality, the sexual act, sexual power, death, dying, rebirth, explosions, power struggles . . . you get the idea.

The world events surrounding its discovery included two world wars, the emergence of atomic weapons, the rise of Nazis and Hitler, concentration camps, and the annihilation of six million Jews and minority groups. It also saw the birth of psychoanalysis, notably the work of Sigmund Freud, which focuses on sexuality, and Carl Jung, whose work deals with mythology, dreams, archetypes, and synchronicity. So what kind of archetype might be emerging with the *rediscovery* of Ophiuchus?

Well, it's the only astrological sign based on a real person: Asclepius. By the ancient Greeks in 27 B.C. he was regarded as a healer, and in the Roman pantheon he is a son of Apollo. He supposedly learned the secrets of preventing death when he observed one serpent bringing healing herbs to another. He raised the dead using this herb. In order to prevent the entire human race from becoming immortal under his care, Zeus supposedly killed him with a bolt of lightning, then later suffered a pang of conscience and placed his image in the heavens to honor his good works.

Ophiuchus is usually depicted as grasping a snake—thus his name as the Serpent Bearer—and has one foot resting firmly against Scorpius (the scorpion). In honor of Asclepius, snakes were often used in healing rituals, and nonvenomous snakes were allowed to crawl on the floor in dormitories where the sick and injured slept. Cults grew up around Asclepius in Greece and Rome, and pilgrims supposedly flocked to his healing temples from 300 B.C. onward. Ritual purification would be followed by offerings or sacrifices to the gods and by spending the night in the holiest part of the sanctuary so that dreams would occur. Any dreams or visions were reported to a priest, who would prescribe the appropriate therapy by interpreting what the dreams meant.

Just from the mythology we can glimpse some of the components of the archetype: healer, alternative medicine, the power of groups (pilgrims flocking to the temples), magic (raising the dead), dream interpretation, cult mentality, violence and violent deaths, sudden unexpected events (thunderbolts), resisting and questioning authority, pushing against the status quo, a greater independence from authoritarian rule (sounds like what has been going on in Egypt and the Middle East and North Africa in general), and greater dependence on the self and the local community.

Other components of this archetype include what author and physician Dean Radin calls "the global mind, the collective consciousness of everyone on the planet." This phrase grew out of Radin's involvement in the Global Consciousness Project. In 1998 Princeton's Dr. Roger Nelson, in conjunction with the Institute of Noetic Sciences, began an Internet-based experiment aimed at monitoring this global mind. Through dozens of random number generators situated worldwide, the idea is that "as mind moves, so does matter" (Dean Radin). The findings so far are intriguing.

Networks of random number generators are present at sixty-five sites worldwide. Once a minute the generated numbers are downloaded and analyzed for consistency. The process is explained in detail on the project's Web site: www.gcpdot.com. The purpose of the project, according to the Web site, is "to examine subtle correlations that may reflect the presence and activity of consciousness in the world. We predict structure in what should be random data, associated with major world events."

So during events that are of global interest, the focused attention and emotional outpouring worldwide brings about a notable difference in the results. The Web site maintains a GCP dot that registers these fluctuations in the global mind in real time, covered 24/7 by the media. Hours before the first plane hit the World Trade Center, these random number generators went a bit nuts, and the button turned red. If you read what it says about colors on the Global Consciousness Project Web site, you'll see that red indicates a variance in the statistical analysis of these generators—an event that mass consciousness registers, sometimes before the event occurs it seems. The same thing happened during the original O.J. Simpson trial and shortly before the Tucson shootings involving Representative Gabrielle Giffords earlier this year. In other words, these generators registered the fluctuations in consciousness.

Magnetic fluctuation impacts human beings, and it may be creating a sensitivity in certain types of individuals, which is part of this emerging paradigm. Planetary empaths are individuals who seem to be so intimately connected to fluctuations in the earth that they experience physical symptoms for days and sometimes weeks before a natural disaster occurs. Their "symptoms" are astonishingly similar and often coincide with the change in colors in the GCP dot. One woman in California, for instance, knows that when her left ear starts ringing and throbbing painfully, an earthquake is imminent. Another woman is seized by vertigo before a quake.

There's no question a paradigm shift of some sort is underway. This shift in mass consciousness may be what the rediscovery of Ophiuchus presages.

That said, there are troubling facts emerging that suggest this paradigm shift may occur *as a result of* global warming, an increase in natural disasters, a widening disparity between rich and poor, and increased political and religious strife worldwide. We've covered some of the facts in other posts—about the massive deaths of birds and other wildlife, for instance. Here are some additional facts:

- In 2010 natural disasters killed more than a quarter of a million people and displaced millions. According to Swiss Re, the largest reinsurer in the world, the financial losses from these natural disasters exceeded two hundred and twenty-two billion dollars.
- Greenland's ice sheet melted at a record rate in 2010.
- 2005 and 2010 are tied for the warmest years on record.
- The last pole shift occurred nearly 800,000 years ago. Some scientists believe we're long overdue. Others believe a pole shift is already underway.

So this rediscovery of Ophiuchus may be a warning, or it may be prompting us to really examine our collective beliefs and desires. What do we *want* not only for ourselves and our loved ones, but for the planet?

CHAPTER 11

The Astro Neighborhood

If you Google *astrology*, more than 40 million links show up. Perhaps in uncertain times people are looking for information and insights through nontraditional sources. Or maybe astrology has gone mainstream!

You can find sites for virtually any aspect of this fascinating field, but some sites are far superior and more user friendly than others. These sites offer free natal charts, daily transits, monthly horoscopes, and political and world predictions. It's all at your fingertips. Here are the sites we consider to be the best:

www.astrologyzone.com: Susan Miller's site is a favorite for neophytes and pros alike. Every month she writes about 3,000 words per sign, with detailed predictions for the month. She cites the best days for romance, finances, and career matters. She discusses new and full moons, eclipses and their impact on your sun sign, and provides information on various aspects that are coming up in a given month. You can also obtain a free natal chart. Her site is chocked with information and is user friendly, and her predictions are eerily accurate.

www.astro.com: This site is also jammed with information. Here you can get a free natal chart, see immediately where the planets are today, use the ephemeris, and find out the geographical coordinates for a particular city. There are other interesting tidbits as well—celebrities born on a given day and fascinating and informative articles by some of the world's best astrologers. This site is perfect for the beginner, the intermediary, and the advanced astrologer.

www.moonvalleyastrologer.com: Celeste Teal is *the* expert on eclipses, a specialized area of astrology that few have researched the way she has. Her two books on eclipses are seminal works. She also provides informative articles on various aspects of astrology. If you're new to astrology, there's plenty on this site to whet your appetite. Regardless of your expertise in astrology, Celeste's site offers information for everyone.

www.astrocollege.com: Lois Rodden's site is extraordinary. This woman spent most of her life collecting birth data and then created a piece of software that is invaluable in research. For example, you can compare charts of individuals in virtually any field and discover what astrological components they have in common. Let's say you're looking for artists who all had Leo suns, Capricorn moons, and Scorpio rising. You enter those criteria, and the software delivers names. The software also provides *signatures*—a certain combination of aspects and other factors that point to particular characteristics in an individual. In addition, the site rates and sells astrology software. Lois has passed on, but her work survives.

http://astrofuturetrends.com: Author and astrologer Anthony Louis does just what the site says. He predicts future trends, covers political stuff, and provides an overall view of astrology.

www.starlightnews.com: Click on Nancy's blog. Here you'll find the latest predictions and insights about world affairs. Nancy's predictions about politics have been right on. Before the 2004 election she made some predictions about tight senatorial races that were totally accurate. She also called the presidential race in 2008. We've been following her closely ever since. She receives hundreds of comments for her posts, and some of them are as informative as her posts.

www.ofscarabs.blogspot.com: About synchronicities— what they are, how they show up in our lives, what they might mean, and hundreds of stories. There are occasional posts on astrological factors, like Mercury retrograde!

Software

In the days before computers a natal chart or anything else connected to astrology had to be configured manually, through complicated mathematical formulas that left you gasping. Astrology software has truly transformed the study of astrology and our knowledge about it. Since the late 1980s, when we began using astrology software, the choices have multiplied.

Our first piece of software was a really simple program we found at a computer store for ten bucks. It erected a chart in about sixty seconds. There it was, rising, moon, sun, planets, the houses, everything set up on the computer screen as if by magic. In the late

1990s we bought our first really terrific astrology software from Matrix for about $300. In the years since http://www.astrologysoftware.com has supplied us with endless data and information and revolutionized the study of astrology.

But it's not just enough to have a great piece of software. When your computer crashes, when you receive updates that screw up, when windows updates to a new system, you call the Matrix help line, and their people walk you through it until everything works. And the employees on their help lines aren't outsourced. You won't reach India. You'll talk to someone in Michigan who is not only an astrologer, but a computer geek who knows how to fix your problem. If by some fluke they can't fix your problem, they'll credit you for one of their other terrific programs.

The only complaint we have about Matrix is that to activate the software, you have to call or contact them through the Internet to receive a special code. If your computer crashes, if you buy a new PC or laptop . . . well, it's annoying. When you pay this much for software, you shouldn't have to obtain a special access code.

Another great piece of software is **SolarFire**. Astrologers are as dedicated to this program as they are to Matrix's software. Check out http://www.alabe.com for current prices. While the two programs offer similar features and capabilities, preferences seem to be individual. Both Matrix's Winstar and astrolabe's SolarFire offer many of the same features—natal charts, transits, progressed charts, solar charts, and interpretations. They both feature material about fixed stars, aspects, lunations, eclipses, and all the other important components you could possibly want or need. The main difference lies in the appearance of the charts and how the information is presented.

Kepler's astrology program—http://www.astrosoftware.com—is beautiful in its rendition of charts, interpretations, and just about anything any astrologer could use or need. We like it for its ease, its beauty. But it lacks the complexity of both Winstar and SolarFire. The program simply doesn't do as much.

If your exploration of astrology takes you deeper, there are other software programs that help get you there. Bernadette Brady is the undisputed mistress of fixed stars. Her software program, *Starlight*, is remarkable not only for its accuracy but for its presentation. You will never think of fixed stars in the same way once you play with this program. What won't make sense in a natal chart interpretation suddenly snaps into clarity when you use her software. Be sure to download a print to file version for the software—through a PDF file—so that you can maximize usage. Their website: http://www.zyntara.com.

Lois Rodden's AstroDatabank is the software that Lois Rodden developed. It contains over 30,000 birth records, "carefully documented and coded for accuracy with the popular Rodden Rating system. Astro-Databank includes intriguing biographies, revealing personality traits, important life events, and significant relationships." For the curious, the researcher, the neophyte, and pro alike.

Both Winstar and SolarFire produce computerized report software. These reports are handy for when a friend of a friend is in a fix, and you don't have the time to interpret transits and progressions for the person's birth chart. Winstar also produces software on other divination systems.

Day Watch, another Winstar program, is forecasting software that is invaluable for astrologers. From their site: "Certainly it creates personalized astrological calendars, a great tool for professional astrologers and those who have an understanding of astrological terms, symbols, and technique. But Day Watch also contains a full range of onscreen and printable interpretations of events that even someone with absolutely no astrological training can read, understand, and immediately put to use in their daily lives."

Io/Edition Graphic Astrology is the only astrology software for Macs. It's basic, but better than not having any software at all.

At the beginning of every month we bring up our personalized calendars, which tell us what is happening daily in our natal charts and also lists which planets are changing signs in that month, on what date, and which planets are turning retrograde or direct. Each month includes an ephemeris and lunar charts for the new and full moon. The program also offers various types of reports.

Getting a Reading

So now you're ready for an astrological reading. But where do you start? Which astrologer should you use?

The best way to find an astrologer is through someone who has gotten a reading and recommends the individual. If you don't know anyone who has had an astrological reading, then the next best course is to head over to the nearest bookstore and look through the astrology books. Browse through titles that interest you. Note the author's style. If the author uses a lot of astro jargon or seems to write in a depressing or heavy-handed way, move on. Once you find an author whose book you like, check to see if he or she has a Web site. Most astrologers these days have Web sites that spell out their fees, what types of readings are offered, and a contact address.

Rates for a reading vary from one astrologer to another and usually depend on what you want. Would you like just an interpretation of your natal chart? Would you like a forecast for the next six months or a year? Do you want a compatibility chart for you and your partner? Some astrologers prefer to do phone readings, and record the reading. Others prefer to work through e-mail. If the astrologer you've chosen lives close to you, all the better. Have the reading done in person.

What to Expect During a Reading

Every astrological reading begins with your natal chart, so an accurate birth time is essential. It should come from your birth certificate or a parent's memory. An approximate time means the entire reading won't be as accurate. Over the years we've done way too many readings that turned out to be based on inaccurate birth times and then had to construct an accurate chart. If you don't know your time of birth, it's possible to rectify your chart based on major events in your life—the date of your marriage or divorce, a major move, the death of a parent. But this process is time consuming and rarely as accurate as an exact birth time.

A reading with an astrologer differs from a daily horoscope you find in a newspaper or even on a Web site. It's tailored to your specific chart rather than just to your sun sign. If you're getting a reading only on your birth chart, then the astrologer interprets the entire chart, not just pieces of it. The astrologer looks at the signs and house placements of the various planets and the angles the planets make to each other.

If you want predictions for the next six or twelve months, the astrologer uses various techniques that are all based on your natal chart. Transits—the daily motion of the planets—have the most immediate impact on our lives, so the astrologer will first look at how the slower-moving planets (Pluto, Neptune, Uranus) impact your chart. Since they stay in the same sign for the greatest length of time, their influence can be felt for decades. The transits of the other planets are also taken into account, of course. Usually the astrologer will pay close attention to how the transits of your chart's ruler are affecting you. If you have Scorpio rising, then the transits of Pluto and Mars (the coruler) would be important. If you have Gemini rising, then Mercury's transits would be important. The astrologer should also consider how eclipses and the new and full moons might affect you, particularly when there's a lunation in the same sign as your natal sun, moon, or rising.

Another predictive technique the astrologer should use is one called progression. In this technique your natal chart is progressed forward in time to the present. Since the moon is the swiftest-moving planet, moving about one progressed degree a month, the progressed chart provides timing. An astrologer can time events down to a month.

Yet another predictive technique is called the solar return chart, where your sun sign is returned to where it was at your birth. This chart's influence extends from one birthday to the next and when compared with the natal chart provides additional information and insights about what you can expect during the next twelve months.

An astrologer may also take a look at other elements in your chart or, if you have a specific question, can erect an horary chart for that particular question. Horary astrology is a specialized field, and not all astrologers are competent to answer questions using this technique.

CHAPTER 12

By the Numbers

Even though this is an astrology book, we use numbers in some of the daily predictions because we're attempting to remain true to what Sydney Omarr did. The legendary astrologer was also a numerologist and combined the two forms in his work. So let's take a closer look at how the numbers work.

If you're familiar with numerology, you probably know your life path number, which is derived from your birth date. That number represents who you were at birth and the traits that you'll carry throughout your life. There are numerous books and Web sites that provide details on what the numbers mean regarding your life path.

But in the daily predictions, what does it mean when it's a number 9 day, and how did it get to be that number? In the dailies you'll usually find these numbers on the days when the moon is transiting from one sign to another. The system is simple: add the numbers related to the astrological sign (1 for Aries, 2 for Taurus, etc.), the year, the month, and the day.

For example, to find what number June 14, 2011, is

for a Libra, you would start with 7, the number for Libra, add 4 (the number you get when you add 2011 together), plus 6 for June, plus 5 (1+4) for the day. That would be 7+4+6+5 (sign + year + month+ day) = 22=4. So June 14, 2011, is a number 4 day for a Libra. It would be a 5 day for a Scorpio, the sign following Libra. So on that number 4 day, Libra might be advised that her organizational skills are highlighted, that she should stay focused, get organized, be methodical and thorough. She's building a creative future. Tear down the old in order to rebuild. Keep your goals in mind; follow your ideas.

Briefly, here are the meanings of the numbers, which are included in more detail in the dailies themselves.

1) Taking the lead, getting a fresh start, a new beginning
2) Cooperation, partnership, a new relationship, sensitivity
3) Harmony, beauty, pleasures of life, warm, receptive
4) Getting organized, hard work, being methodical, rebuilding, fulfilling your obligations
5) Freedom of thought and action, change, variety, thinking outside the box
6) A service day, being diplomatic, generous, tolerant, sympathetic
7) Mystery, secrets, investigations, research, detecting deception, exploration of the unknown, of the spiritual realms
8) Your power day, financial success, unexpected money, a windfall

9) Finishing a project, looking beyond the immediate, setting your goals, reflection, expansion.

Simple, right?

Once you become accustomed to what the numbers mean for a particular day, you can adjust your attitude and thoughts accordingly. After all, how a day or week, month or year unfolds depends more on your attitude toward yourself and your world than it does on any number or astrology sign. If you practice waking up each morning in a spirit of adventure and gratitude, then pretty soon it becomes second nature, and your life shifts accordingly. Sound like magical thinking? It is. Try it, and watch your life change.

CHAPTER 13

Romance and Timing for Libra in 2013

For the Single Libra

Imagine if you had a genie in a bottle who could grant your every wish, who could tell you when, where, and how you would meet your soul mate. Astrology may not be able to grant your every wish, but it can certainly pinpoint time frames that are favorable for romance and love, getting engaged or married, moving, selling your home, starting a new job. In terms of romance and love we look to the transits of Venus first.

Venus, as the planet that symbolizes love, romance, the arts, creativity, and money, is considered, along with Jupiter, to be one of the beneficial planets. So we look at the signs and houses it transits and whether it's making a harmonious or challenging angle to your sun and other planets. We also look at Mars, symbolic of your sexual and physical energy, and Mercury, symbolic of communication. We examine the signs and houses they are transiting and the angles they're making to other planets. We look for propitious new and full moons and also take into account what the larger planets are doing.

So let's take a closer look at the dates to watch for in 2013 that favor romance, love, and creative endeavors.

August 16 to September 11. Venus is in your sign, and with it comes renewed self-confidence, a feeling that anything is possible, and a general sense of optimism. These feelings can be self-fulfilling. In fact, the more feelings you have like this, the more likely it is that you'll attract someone who interests you romantically. Your presence appeals to others; people everywhere are open to you and your ideas. Open the front door to your social life during this period—accept invites for parties, dinners, concerts, get out and be seen. As always, balance will be key to your passions during this time. Be careful that you don't bend over backward to please the new person in your life.

It's a favorable time to pitch your ideas at work, land a promotion and raise, submit manuscripts, photos, music, to take steps with your creative passions. Your muse is at your beck and call, Libra.

February 1 to 25. During this period Venus is in that area of your chart that symbolizes romance, love, creativity, and children—your solar fifth house. It's one of the most romantic and creative periods for you all year. With Venus in visionary Aquarius, your emotions may be way outside your usual box, which is fine. You're ready to attract someone unusual and embrace the unknown.

If you're uninvolved at the beginning of the transit, you probably won't be when the transit ends. But if you are, it won't make much difference. You're having too much fun and are deeply involved in creative projects and travel.

May 9 to June 2. Venus transits Gemini and your solar ninth house. Romance may find you while you're traveling, taking a course or workshop, or even while you're involved in spiritual work. Your intuition should be strong now. Heed it; it won't steer you wrong.

For the Partnered Libra

Whether you and your partner are married, living together, or just getting to know each other, the above dates should be beneficial for the relationship. Let's find out how.

August 16 to September 11. With Venus in your sign, your self-confidence is humming along at a perfect pitch, and others find your presence intriguing, attractive. Others like your ideas, everything you have to say. You and your partner should be seeing eye to eye on most things, and when you don't, you just shrug it off and wait for another day. Or, at any rate, that's what you should do. But the drawback to this transit is that you may be too eager to keep the peace, to please, and bend like a flower in the wind.

February 1 to 25. During Venus' transit of Aquarius and your solar fifth house you discover your capacity for love, being romanced, joining with your partner in a creative project of some kind. During this period your mind must be seduced with ideas, beauty, the unusual. Once your mind is seduced, your heart follows. You and your partner enjoy the sensual pleasures of your relationship. You and your partner spend time doing what you both enjoy.

Between **December 21 and January 30** Venus is retrograde in Capricorn, which suggests there could be some bumps and bruises on the home front.

May 9 to June 2. You and your partner may take off for parts unknown. The journey can be literal or figurative, in that you explore some sort of mystery or perhaps join up for a creative project. Your communication should be exceptionally good.

For All Libras

Venus and Mars. Female and male. Anima and animus. Love and sex. These two planets have a lot to tell us about our psychological makeup when it comes to relationships.

Venus represents our capacity for love, how we are romantic and creative, and what we're looking for in an intimate relationship. Every Venus transit accentuates a different part of our romantic souls. During a Venus transit in a sign that has the same element as your sun sign—air for you, Libra—the qualities of that element are heightened. You feel more attractive, self-confident, optimistic, enthusiastic, social, communicative. Venus in a fellow air sign enables you to make friends with just about anyone. Your enthusiasm, artistic sensibilities, and romantic soul shine forth.

Mars symbolizes our physical energy, aggression, sexuality. So when Mars is in an air sign, your physical and sexual energy are excellent. You're ready to take on the world.

Here are the dates when Mars is in an air sign:

May 31 to July 13. During this period Mars is in Gemini, your solar ninth house. This transit increases your urge to travel and express yourself, and you feel invigorated, grounded.

December 7 to July 25. Mars transits your sign! This period is when you should really be in your element. Your physical and sexual energy are superb, and you pursue what and who you desire. If you're involved in a relationship already, then things should move along at a pace that suits you. This transit brings your energy and focus to romance, love, creativity. If you and your partner have thought about starting a family, then pregnancy could occur during this transit. However, Mars will be retrograde between March 1 and May 19, 2014, and that's when the energy turns inward.

Other Important Dates

We talk about new and full moons elsewhere in the book, but in terms of love, romance, and sex, here are some dates to circle:

February 10, new moon in fellow air sign Aquarius. This one brings in new opportunities for love, romance, creative projects. It favors starting a family, if you're so inclined!

June 8, new moon in Gemini. Put on your traveling shoes, Libra. This new moon may bring new opportunities for foreign travel. Some new opportunity in communication may surface as well.

October 4, new moon in your sign. This new moon

occurs just once a year. It ushers in new personal opportunities that should please you. Plan for it by creating a wish board of your desires. Back your desires with emotion. Post your wish board where you'll see it often. Trust that the universe will make things happen.

♎ CHAPTER 14

Your Spirituality in 2013

Neptune is so far out there in space that it's invisible without a telescope. It took Voyager 2 twelve years just to reach the planet. Its atmosphere is composed of hydrogen, helium, and frozen methane, which gives Neptune's clouds their blue color. These clouds zip around the planet at speeds of up to 700 miles an hour. The planet's diameter at the equator is almost four times that of Earth. It's nearly seventeen times as massive, but less dense than our planet.

In astrology Neptune represents what is hidden, veiled, mysterious. It rules ghosts, hauntings, illusions, and spiritual insights and stimulates imagination, artistic inspiration, flashes of genius, and all that is mystical. It also symbolizes your personal unconscious. On the down side, it represents delusion, escapism, addiction of all kinds, deception. It's the natural ruler of Pisces and the twelfth house. Neptune takes about fourteen years to move through a sign and roughly 168 years to move through the zodiac. Only Pluto moves more slowly. Its impact, then, is felt over time, in subtle ways.

In February 2012 it entered Pisces, the sign it rules, where it will be for the next fourteen years. During this long transit Neptune is in your solar sixth house. This house rules your daily work routine, the maintenance of your daily health.

During this transit you may be seeking ways to integrate your spirituality and ideals more readily into your daily work life. There could be some confusion with employees or coworkers, perhaps because boundaries between you and them are blurred. There can also be deep spiritual connections with the people with whom you work.

If you have any health issues during this period, seek a second and even a third diagnosis. Neptune's transit through this house can make health problems difficult to diagnose correctly.

The Pisces part of the transit increases your imagination and deepens your intuition, and you may feel a need to integrate your ideals and spiritual beliefs more readily into the rest of your life. Your dreams should be amazingly vivid during this transit, and with a little practice you can easily become proficient at recalling them and gleaning insights and information from them. You may get involved in charity work or could volunteer for an animal shelter, a community center, a homeless shelter. Since Neptune is forming a challenging angle to your sun, you may experience some of the negatives of this transit. Later in this chapter we'll provide suggestions for mitigating the confusion and getting the most out of this transit.

Dates to Watch For

Between **February 25 and March 21** Venus will be traveling with Neptune in Pisces. During this period your spiritual connection with a partner could deepen considerably. The duo of Venus and Neptune should be quite pleasant for your love life, particularly if the spiritual connection is there too.

It could be that you have psychic experiences while these two planets travel together. If so, they should be interesting and insightful, nothing to be afraid of.

On **March 11** the new moon in Pisces will usher in new partnership opportunities. You and your romantic interest may decide to deepen your commitment to each other by getting engaged, moving in together, or getting married. You may embark on a joint creative project.

On the day of that new moon six planets will be in Pisces, with Neptune and Mercury traveling very closely together. So around this time you may be discussing or writing about your spiritual beliefs, imagination, partnerships, or creative endeavors. You might join an online discussion group or forum concerning spirituality or psychic phenomena. Or you may start blogging about your experiences.

June 6 to November 13. Neptune will be retrograde in Pisces. This movement tends to drive your searching inward. You may be taking a closer look at your partnership needs.

If you've always had a yearning to write a book, the new moon in Pisces could bring the imaginative nudge you need to get started. With Neptune in Pisces, you can easily write from an inspired place within yourself. Neptune rules our higher minds, the part of us that is connected to what Esther and Jerry Hicks call Source energy, to the divine, to the part of us that is larger, vaster, wiser.

Synchronicity and Neptune

Synchronicity, a term coined by Carl Jung, is the coming together of inner and outer events in a way that can't be explained by cause and effect and is meaningful to the observer. Meaningful coincidences. You may experience a lot of these during Neptune's transit through Pisces.

Synchronicities can involve anything. You might be driving along, thinking about a particular person or issue and then hear something on the car radio that seems to address that very individual or issue. These experiences often act as wakeup calls that open you to a greater reality, to the realization that we are all connected, that what affects one affects all. Once you become aware of meaningful coincidences, you'll notice that they often manifest themselves through global events. Then it's as if the universe is addressing us as a collective—as people of the same country, continent, world. The oil spill in the Gulf of Mexico certainly qualifies as a global synchronicity.

On March 31, 2010, President Obama unveiled a sweeping plan to open up the eastern Gulf of Mexico, the south Atlantic coast, and areas off northern Alaska to new oil and gas exploration. As noted in the St. Petersburg *Times*, "Never mind that the eastern gulf has less oil than America consumes in a year. Any supplies would not make a dent in the price of fuel at the pump. But moving the boundary east would shift the next fight over drilling even closer to land."

Just twenty days later, on April 20, a BP oil rig exploded in the gulf, just fifty miles off the Louisiana coast, killing eleven people and creating what has become the worst oil spill in history. On the day of the explosion BP executives were on the rig, celebrating their safety record. It was as if the universe said, *Safety record? Are you kidding? I don't think so, boys.*

Synchronicities often involve clusters—of numbers, names, objects, virtually anything. A common cluster of numbers involves 11, 111, 11:11. One day, for example, when we were working on a chapter in our book, *7 Secrets of Synchronicity*, we received a bill from our daughter's college for the year-end cleaning of the dorm suite she shared with three other women. The charge was $111 and loose change.

That same day, in the midst of corresponding with people on our blog (www.synchrosecrets.com/synchrose crets), we took a break so Rob could pick up our car from the shop. It had just gotten its second alternator in two weeks. He drove away from the garage at 3:17 P.M. and looked down at the dashboard clock to see if it registered the same time as his watch. But because the battery had been disconnected, the clock had stopped. The time? 11:11.

Jung believed that repeated clusters of a number mean that number has become active in your psyche. So if you experience clusters of numbers—or anything else, for that matter—do some research on it. Clusters of 11s, for instance, tend to occur during periods of heightened awareness. Psychic Uri Geller, who writes extensively about this cluster on his Web site, considers 11:11 to be a doorway, "a crack between two worlds . . . a bridge which has the inherent potential of linking together two very different spirals of energy."

Neptune in Pisces heightens your awareness of underlying patterns, and synchronicity is all about repeating patterns. You may want to keep a journal about your synchronicity experiences. Over time you'll be able to decipher the message of your synchronicities more quickly and accurately. Keep in mind that synchronicities can originate in dreams, usually as precognitive or telepathic information.

Neptune will be retrograde between June 6 and November 13. During this period your inward seeking will be intense.

Suggestions

With Neptune in Pisces forming a challenging angle to your sun, here are some suggestions to mitigate the negatives of this transit:

- Moderation in all substances. It's too easy to fall into the escapist part of Neptune's transit—alcohol, drugs, food binges. The same goes for your partner.
- Take up meditation and yoga. Both will help to ground you. If you can talk your partner into doing the same, even better!
- Check your hunches against the facts.

- Try not to be needy.
- Don't allow yourself to fall into a victim mentality.
- Don't allow others to take advantage of you.
- Explore your ideals and how you might integrate them more readily into your life.
- Take classes in intuitive development.
- Learn to recall your dreams and request information and insights about things that concern you.
- In addition to yoga, establish a regular exercise routine if you don't have one already. Exercise will help you to burn off your enormous physical energy.
- Pay close attention to what you eat. If possible, stick to fresh fruits and vegetables and go organic!
- Heed the synchronicities in your experience. Decipher their messages.

CHAPTER 15

Navigating Saturn in 2013 for Libra

Without Saturn in the grand astrological scheme of things, our universe would be formless, just a swirling soup of potential. Keep that in mind the next time you're ranting about your responsibilities and delays and restrictions in some area of your life. If you feel put upon, if you feel that you're the one in your office always doing most of the work, if you feel you haven't been duly recognized by bosses and peers, a partner, even your kids, then chances are good that you're going through a difficult Saturn transit.

Saturn doesn't provide any free rides. Whatever this planet brings into your life, it's because you've earned it—in this life or another. The areas this planet rules reflect its stern nature. It's a school marm, shaking its finger in your face, reminding you to live up to your responsibilities, to be disciplined in what you do, to erect solid, durable structures in your life. Limitations, delays, and restrictions also fall under Saturn's rule. So do teeth and bones. It's known as the planet of karma.

Where it appears in your birth chart is the area

where you will learn responsibility. Saturn shows us our limitations, and through it we learn the rules of the game here in physical reality.

This planet takes about two and a half years to transit a sign and about twenty-nine years to move through the zodiac. Each sign, every angle it forms to your sun, teaches you something different. Every twenty-nine years, however, you experience a Saturn return, when the planet returns to where it was when you were born. The first one happens around the age of twenty-nine, the second one when you're between the ages of fifty-eight and sixty, and the third one, if you live long enough, around the age of ninety. These returns are major turning points in life.

At the first Saturn return you get married or divorced, start a family, embark on a career, go to graduate school. You get the idea. These events are major transitions that pivot your life in new directions.

At your second Saturn return the events are no less dramatic, but you're older and more seasoned, in a better place to put them into the larger context of your life. This is when people retire, care for aging parents, become empty-nesters, downsize, and even sometimes start new careers, doing what they love and have postponed for years.

The third Saturn return seems to be one of reflection. It's when you appreciate the life you have lived, forgive yourself and others, find satisfaction in what you have accomplished, and gain a deeper understanding of where you have been, who you are, and where you are going. The third return may also be when, at some level, you begin to plan for your next life.

Saturn in 2013

On October 5, 2012, Saturn left Libra and entered Scorpio, where it will be until December 24, 2014, when it will enter Sagittarius. In mid-June 2015 Saturn will dip back into Scorpio, but in September 2015 it will reenter Sagittarius, where it will be until late December 2017. For you, Saturn's transit through Scorpio should be good. The transit through Sadge may be more challenging.

During Saturn's transit through Scorpio, your solar second house, your conscious mind seeks depth, your values deepen. There could be delays with finances and income and restrictions concerning your spending. Any research and investigations you conduct will be done thoroughly, efficiently. Your relationships with others may change significantly, but at subtle levels. You may consider starting a blog or building a Web site about a topic that interests you or to promote a service or product.

In terms of romantic and business relationships, you walk away from whatever is shallow. Your emotions are more intense and powerful enough to move mountains. Later in the chapter we'll talk about ways to enhance the energies of this transit so that you benefit fully.

Whenever Scorpio is part of the astrological equation, you may be delving more deeply into the unseen side of life, into all that is mysterious—ghosts, hauntings, orbs, synchronicities that involve dreams, communication with the dead, precognitive information, memories of past lives. Or you may undertake that exploration with a friend, sibling, or other relative.

Good books for this transit? Anything by author Jane Roberts, who for years channeled Seth, "a personality essence no longer focused in physical existence." The twenty or so books that Roberts channeled covered the gamut of esoteric topics. Other recommendations: *The Holographic Universe* by Michael Talbot, anything by Esther and Jerry Hicks, *Children's Past Lives* by Carol Bowman.

Dates to Watch For

April 25. Lunar eclipse in Scorpio. Intense emotions swirl around and within you. Transformation in your finances should be positive. Your passions run high. Saturn is close to this eclipse degree, suggesting a seriousness to any news you hear.

January 1 to June 25. Jupiter transits air sign Gemini and your solar ninth house and forms a beneficial angle to your sun. This one brings tremendous expansion in your worldview, spiritual beliefs, and understanding of other cultures.

June 25, 2013 to July 16, 2014. Jupiter transits Cancer and your career area. Buckle up, Libra. Professional options multiply. Jupiter forms a beneficial angle to Saturn in Scorpio, so your intuition deepens, particularly about professional matters.

Look at your natal chart to find out where Gemini and Cancer fall. These are the areas of your life that experience the greatest expansion during Jupiter's transits through Gemini and Cancer.

November 3. The solar eclipse in Scorpio features five planets in this sign, including Saturn. This one is apt to be intense and powerful and impacts your finances—what you earn and spend as well as your partner's earnings and things like mortgages and loans.

August 16 to September 11. Venus transits your sign, making this period one of the most romantic and creative all year. Others find you appealing, seductive, charming. You may be more discriminating about matters of the heart because you have a clear idea what you're looking for in a partner.

December 7 to July 26, 2014. Mars transits Libra. This one is your booster rocket. You're physically charged up, ready to go, and nothing will hold you back. Your sexual energy is especially powerful. Your social skills are superb. For part of this transit Mars is retrograde—March 4, 2014, to May 20, 2014.

Meaningful relationships will become a priority when Venus travels with Saturn between **September 11 and October 7.** This period brings a serious tone and texture to any business or romantic partnerships. You and your partner may discover such a deep connection that you take your relationship to the next level. Or, equally possible, you discover the darker sides of Scorpio—envy, jealousy, possessiveness, manipulation—and decide to end things.

Between **September 29 and October 21** Mercury, planet of communication and travel, joins Saturn in Scorpio. This transit brings greater depth to your conscious mind. You are more intuitive, perhaps more secretive, but are looking for the absolute bottom line in everything you do, feel, investigate, and think. You will expect complete honesty in all your dealings with people. Be prepared to offer the same.

Suggestions

- Don't take the easy way out in anything you do.
- Establish a schedule for your creative work. Stick to it. During your creativity time, let your imagination wander freely.
- Establish a regular exercise regimen. Join a gym, take up yoga.
- Meditate.
- Explore your feelings and be willing to communicate what you feel.
- Be alert for synchronicities—meaningful coincidences. These synchronicities can be guide posts, signs along the path of your life that point you in a particular direction. They can act as confirmation, warnings, reassurance.
- Ask for guidance in your dreams—Neptune in Pisces should help in that regard.
- Take a workshop in intuitive development, alternative healing, or something creative that interests you.
- Read, read, read.
- Start a blog.
- Create a space in your home to which you can retreat when you feel overwhelmed.
- Be conscious about your nutrition—conscious, not obsessive.
- Pat yourself on the back whenever you do something well!
- Practice appreciating everything in your environment.

♎ CHAPTER 16

Using Pluto to Your Advantage in 2013

Pluto lost its status as a planet on August 24, 2006. On that day the International Astronomical Union voted to demote Pluto to a dwarf planet. It apparently doesn't meet the three conditions necessary for a celestial body to be considered a planet:

- The body must orbit a star.
- It must be massive enough for its own gravity to pull it into a nearly spherical shape.
- The object has "cleared the neighborhood" around its orbit.

Pluto meets the first two criteria. The third criterion is where Pluto failed. According to infoplease. com, ". . . the other planets have either assimilated or repulsed most other objects in their orbits, and each has more mass than the combined total of everything else in its area." Pluto is just one of numerous objects in its orbit.

However, to astrologers it remains a powerful force in the zodiac. Discovered in 1930, Pluto is the most distant planet from the sun, invisible to us except through a telescope. It exists at the edge of the solar system, its light so dim it seems etheric. It takes 248 years to make a circuit of the zodiac, i.e., it moves like a snail! But this slow movement is what makes its transits so powerful.

This small, potent celestial body represents profound, irrevocable transformation. When it entered Capricorn in 2008, it began to bring about change from the bottom up in government, authority figures, and corporate entities that are "too big to fail" and started exposing the dark underbelly of corruption and greed.

Pluto's last transit through Capricorn occurred between November 1762 and December 1, 1778. Let's take a closer look at what was going on then for patterns we may experience globally during its transit now:

- Unrest and outright rebellion and revolution were evident during much of this period in Europe and the colonies.
- Spain acquired Louisiana from France.
- Catherine the Great became empress and presided over wars with the Ottoman Empire.
- Britain struck a deal with Spain to exchange Cuba for Florida.
- The first partition of Poland happened during this period, when that country was divided into three areas owned by Russia, Prussia, and Austria.
- The Quartering Act was passed, requiring the housing of British troops in private homes.

- Parliament passed the Stamp Act, its first serious attempt to assert governmental authority over the colonies. It was intended to pay for the huge national debt Britain had incurred during the Seven Years War, but created a serious threat of revolt.
- The Boston Tea Party occurred during Pluto's last passage through Capricorn.

In other words, dramatic, transformative events occurred, just as they are now. Let's take a closer look at how your life may be impacted and the control you have to turn the tide, if necessary.

Since 2008 Pluto has been moving through your solar fourth house, forming a challenging angle to your sun. This lengthy transit—it lasts until early 2024—alters your home life and domestic situation from the bottom up, the inside out. It may not always be pleasant for you, but Pluto is basically purging your life of what no longer serves your best interests. If you're single, you may get married. If you're married, you could get divorced. If you're happily committed, that probably won't change, and the relationship may be taken to a whole new level.

Important dates to remember:

April 12 to September 20. Pluto is moving retrograde during this period. It means that certain things aren't moving ahead as swiftly as you would like. You may be scrutinizing your deeper goals for 2013 and reassessing your domestic situation and needs.

November 5, 2013, to February 6, 2014. Venus travels with Pluto during this period. The planet's transit usually lasts about three weeks, but it will be retrograde between **December 21, 2013, and January 30, 2014**. When Venus is moving direct, it's a powerful time for love and romance and for creating a home life that suits your deep artistic perceptions. Psychological issues may surface, but that's fine. You welcome self-knowledge. The better you know yourself, the more proficient you become at social interactions.

December 24, 2013, to January 12, 2014. Mercury will be in Capricorn, traveling for a time with both Pluto and Venus. This trio brings deep discussions about your home life, career goals, and deeper needs. There could be some travel during this period, and it's likely it is purely for enjoyment.

Jupiter enters Cancer on **June 25** and will be opposed to Pluto for part of July. Between **July 1 and 21** the opposition could exacerbate tension in some area of your life. You may be prone to blowing things out of proportion and making hasty decisions based on insufficient information. Your emotions will be quite powerful during this period.

January 11 features a new moon in Capricorn with Mercury closely conjunct and Pluto closely conjunct to Mercury, but not to the new moon. Still, because Pluto is involved, any new opportunities that surface are likely to be deeply transformative. Consider them carefully.

Since Pluto in Capricorn forms a challenging angle to your sun, here are some suggestions to bolster its energy so that it works in your favor:

- Make adjustments in your life when necessary. As a cardinal sign, it can be challenging for you to do so, but Pluto won't have it any other way.

- Take time out daily just for yourself. Whether you nap, read a book, drive around, visit friends, shop, or go to the gym, do whatever brings *you* pleasure.
- Establish a regular exercise routine if you don't have one already. Exercise helps to ground you. Your body will come to expect and enjoy it!
- Start meditating. Since your sign is ruled by Venus, which enjoys beauty, you might even have an aesthetically pleasing meditation area with freshly cut flowers, soft lighting, pastel colors. Start small, a few minutes a day. You may surprise yourself and realize that you enjoy it.
- Practice dream recall. Your dreams are great sources of information and insight. Give yourself a suggestion before falling asleep that you'll wake up after an important dream and be able to remember it. Keep your dream journal handy.
- Be mindful of what you eat. Don't eat on the run; try to keep snacks to a minimum. Notice the contents of what you eat. Is the item high in sodium? Fats? Cut out red meats. Go organic when possible.
- Take a seminar or workshop in intuitive development or some other topic that interests you.
- Audition for a part in a play.
- Pluto transits, by their very nature, are intense no matter what sign they're in. Once you've found where Capricorn falls in your natal chart, reread the Houses section in chapter 2 to understand which area of your life will be impacted.

♎ CHAPTER 17

The Big Picture for Libra in 2013

Welcome to 2013! We've covered some of the major transits that will be happening this year and how they'll affect you. So let's look at the inner planets, those that move more swiftly, and see what effects they may have on your life.

Romance/Creativity

Your solar fifth house is Aquarius. This means that any time an inner planet transits that house, things heat up romantically and creatively and with your kids. Your enjoyment becomes paramount. These transits always form beneficial angles to your sun, so it's easier for you to be you!

There are several periods this year when romance and creativity really flow your way. Between August 16 and September 11 Venus transits your sign. This period is remarkably charged with everything that makes you happy. Your self-confidence soars, and others find you enormously appealing and intriguing. Romance, love, and creative endeavors are high on your list of priorities. Just be careful that you don't bend over backward to please a partner.

Between January 19 and February 5 Venus transits Aquarius and your solar fifth house. This period should be the most romantic and creative time for you all year. If you aren't involved when the transit begins, you probably will be by the time it ends. If you're in a relationship, things between you and your partner work flawlessly. The two of you may join on a creative project, and since your muse is at your beck and call 24/7, there's no better time to leap in.

From May 9 to June 2 Venus moves through fellow air sign Gemini and your solar ninth house. This period should be another good one. You and your partner may travel abroad together with the intention of simply enjoying yourselves and exploring places neither of you has been before. You might also take a course or workshop in a topic that interests you both.

Career

In addition to the dates mentioned elsewhere, there are some other stellar dates for professional matters this year. When Venus transits Cancer and your career area between June 2 and 27, it's time to ask for a raise or promotion, pitch ideas, or garner support for a project. There's a certain professional ease with this transit that prompts others to see you as the person with the answers or the wisdom and skills to lead. Venus in Cancer suggests that you'll feel quite intuitive, and that will spill over into your communications and social skills.

Good backup dates? Between May 31 and August 8, Mercury transits Cancer and your career area, an excellent time to discuss and pitch your ideas. You may be hanging out with people from work, brainstorming with them or just socializing. You have a clear sense about what you're doing. Your communication skills are solid, and you're able to translate abstract ideas into practical terms. However, keep in mind that Mercury will be retrograde in Cancer between June 26 and July 20. During that period miscommunication and misunderstandings may be the rule of the day. Don't pitch new ideas or launch new projects. Finish up what you've begun.

Finances

If you have been struck by the downturn in the economy that began in 2008, your financial picture probably should improve this year—if you keep a few simple steps in mind. Between June 25, 2013, and July 16, 2014, expansive Jupiter transits Cancer, your career area, and forms a beneficial angle to your financial house. This transit expands your professional options—a new career path, a new job, a hike in pay, new networks of professional colleagues. So your finances could improve significantly during this transit.

Between January 1 and June 25 Jupiter transits Gemini and your solar ninth house. This period could also prove fruitful in the money department. Your social network expands, and your communication skills broaden. You may be drawn to individuals whose worldview is compatible with your own. These people broaden your understanding of the world in some way. You may be exploring your beliefs about money—how you earn and spend it, how mindful (or not) you are about what you buy and the way you earn your money. New financial opportunities may come through people you meet during this period.

Mercury Retrogrades

Every year Mercury—the planet of communication and travel—turns retrograde three times. During these periods it's wise not to sign contracts (unless you don't mind renegotiating whcn Mercury is moving direct), to check and recheck travel plans, and to communicate as succinctly as possible. Refrain from buying any large-ticket items or electronics during this time too. Often computers and appliances go on the fritz, cars act up, data is lost . . . you get the idea. Be sure to back up all files before the dates below:

February 23–March 17: Mercury is retrograde in Pisces, in your solar sixth house of health and work. Mitigate the effects by communicating clearly with employees and coworkers. If you receive results on any health tests, have the test redone once Mercury is moving direct again.

June 26–July 20: Mercury retrograde in Cancer, your solar tenth house. This one could result in professional snafus. Don't fret about it. Just be up front and honest in your dealings with others.

October 21–November 10: Mercury retrograde in Scorpio, your solar second house. This one impacts your finances—what you earn, what you spend, your values about money and everything else. Double-check all bank statements. Don't apply for a mortgage or loan.

Eclipses

Solar eclipses tend to trigger external events that bring about change according to the sign and house in which they fall. Lunar eclipses trigger inner, emotional events according to the sign and house in which they fall. Any eclipse marks both beginnings and endings. The solar and lunar eclipse in a pair fall in opposite signs. If you're interested in detailed information on eclipses, take a look at Celeste Teal's excellent and definitive book, *Eclipses: Predicting World Events & Personal Transformation.*

If you were born under or around the time of an eclipse, it's to your advantage to take a look at your birth chart to find out exactly where the eclipses will impact you.

Most years feature four eclipses—two solar, two lunar—with the set separated by about two weeks. This year there are three lunar eclipses and two solar eclipses. Let's take a closer look.

April 25: Lunar eclipse in Scorpio. This one should bring financial news and stir up feelings about money. A good time to research and investigate.

May 9: Solar eclipse in Taurus. This eclipse should usher in new opportunities in terms of mortgages, loans, and the investigation of things that go bump in the night. Your partner—or anyone else with whom you share resources—could land a plump raise.

May 25: Lunar eclipse in Sagittarius, your solar third house. This eclipse brings news that impacts your daily life in some way. There could be confusion about the news you hear, so get all your facts before making a decision.

October 18: Lunar eclipse in Aries, your solar seventh house. News and emotions concerning a romantic or business partnership. Venus forms a strong angle to the eclipse degree, so any news you hear is positive.

November 3: Solar eclipse in Scorpio, your solar second house. This one triggers external events related to everything discussed under the April 25 lunar eclipse. Four planets and the North Node are in Scorpio during this eclipse, so get ready for intensity and power.

Luckiest Day of the Year

Every year there's one day when Jupiter and the sun meet up, and luck, serendipity, and expansion are the hallmarks. This year that day falls on June 19, in Gemini. A stellar day! And since it falls in your career area, it should be particularly beneficial professionally.

CHAPTER 18

Eighteen Months of Day-by-Day Predictions: July 2012 to December 2013

Moon sign times are calculated for Eastern Standard Time and Eastern Daylight Time. Please adjust for your local time zone.

JULY 2012

Sunday, July 1 (Moon in Sagittarius) The moon is in your third house today. Take what you know and share it with others. However, keep conscious control of your emotions when getting your ideas across. Your thinking can be unduly influenced by things of the past. Siblings, other relatives, or neighbors play a role. Drive carefully if you're talking on your cell phone as you go about your everyday business.

Monday, July 2 (Moon into Capricorn, 6:52 p.m.) Your charm and wit are appreciated. Your attitude determines everything today. In romance, you're an ardent and loyal lover. Ease up on routines. Remain flexible. Take time to relax, enjoy yourself, recharge your batteries.

Tuesday, July 3 (Moon in Capricorn)   With Mars moving into your first house today, you're quite outgoing and assertive, letting others know exactly what you think and how you feel. Others see you as ambitious. There's also a full moon in your fourth house, and that means you get a better handle on domestic matters. You reap what you've sown.

Wednesday, July 4 (Moon into Aquarius, 8:26 p.m.) Change and variety are highlighted now. Think outside the box. Take risks, experiment. Let go of old structures; get a new point of view. You're especially versatile and changeable today, Libra. Promote new ideas; follow your curiosity.

Thursday, July 5 (Moon in Aquarius)   The moon is in your fifth house today. Your emotions tend to overpower your intellect now. Be yourself; be emotionally honest. In love, there's greater emotional depth to a relationship. It's a good day to take a chance, experiment. Children and animals could play a significant role in your day.

Friday, July 6 (Moon in Aquarius)   You have a greater sense of freedom now. You're dealing with new ideas, new options, originality. You get a new perspective. Play your hunches. Look beyond the immediate. Help others, but dance to your own tune. Your wishes and dreams come true.

Saturday, July 7 (Moon into Pisces, 12:29 a.m.)
It's a power day, and your day to play it your way. Unexpected money arrives. Business discussions go well. It's a good day for buying a lottery ticket. Think big and act big! Be aware that fear of failure or fear that you won't measure up will attract tangible experiences that reinforce the feeling.

Sunday, July 8 (Moon in Pisces)   The moon is in your sixth house today. Others come to you for guidance; you're the "go to" person. They rely on you for information. Help others, but be careful not to fall into a martyr syndrome. Don't forget your own needs. Take care of any health issues. Exercise and watch your diet.

Monday, July 9 (Moon into Aries, 8:14 a.m.)   It's a number 1 day. You get a fresh start now, a new beginning like the phoenix rising from the ashes. Get out and make contacts today. Experiment, explore, discover, and express your opinions. Your originality is highlighted.

Tuesday, July 10 (Moon in Aries)   The moon is in your seventh house today. Make sure that you focus on relationships, business and personal ones. Loved ones and partners play a role. A legal matter comes to your attention. You comprehend the nuances of a situation, but it's difficult to go with the flow.

Wednesday, July 11 (Moon into Taurus, 7:30 p.m.)
Ease up a bit today, Libra. Focus on keeping yourself rather than those around you in balance. You're feel-

ing vital and have a natural ability to express yourself. Your charm and wit are appreciated. You're innovative and communicate well. In romance, you're an ardent and loyal lover.

Thursday, July 12 (Moon in Taurus)   The moon is in your eighth house today. Things could get emotionally intense in your dealings with someone from the opposite sex. That's particularly true if you're facing issues related to shared belongings. You're sensitive and attuned to what's going on around you. You could take an interest in a metaphysical topic, such as past lives.

Friday, July 13 (Moon in Taurus)   Uranus goes retrograde in your seventh house today and stays there until December 13. Your intuitive and inventive nature feels bottled up during the last half of the year. From time to time, the pent-up energy explodes spontaneously, but the results are somewhat erratic. You seek freedom and rebel against all that has held you in place.

Saturday, July 14 (Moon into Gemini, 8:27 a.m.) Mercury goes retrograde in your eleventh house today and stays there until August 8. That means there could be some miscommunication or misunderstanding with friends and associates. Your wishes and dreams are delayed. Leave extra time when traveling. You work for the common good, but others in a group seem to misunderstand your intentions. It will all clear up soon!

Sunday, July 15 (Moon in Gemini)   You're thinking and talking a lot about your philosophy of life, about your ideas on how things should work, about why certain things are happening. You analyze and scrutinize. While you lay it all out for friends or a group, you don't feel much emotional commitment to correcting the situation.

Monday, July 16 (Moon into Cancer, 8:32 p.m.) It's another power day. Unexpected resources come your way. Business discussions go well. You have a chance to expand, to gain recognition, fame, and power. It's a good day to buy a lotto ticket.

Tuesday, July 17 (Moon in Cancer) With the moon in your tenth house today, professional concerns are the focus of the day. You're more responsive to the needs and moods of a group and of the public in general, and more emotional and warm toward co-workers. However, don't blur the boundary between your professional and personal lives.

Wednesday, July 18 (Moon in Cancer) You could be feeling moody today, so it's a good day to work at home, if possible. Water plays a prominent role; you might feel a need to get close to it. Tend to loved ones; do something with them, your children, or sweetheart. You're intuitive and sensitive to other people's moods now.

Thursday, July 19 (Moon into Leo, 6:14 a.m.) There's a new moon in your tenth house today. That means new opportunities come your way related to your profession or career. You get an advancement, a new position, a boost in prestige. It's a good day for sales or dealing with the public.

Friday, July 20 (Moon in Leo)   The moon is in your eleventh house today. Friends play an important role in your day, especially Aquarius and Gemini. You find strength in numbers. You find meaning through friends and groups, especially a group of like-minded people working for the common good.

Saturday, July 21 (Moon into Virgo, 1:25 p.m.) Your organizational skills are highlighted. Control your impulses. Fulfill your obligations. Keep your goals in mind; follow your ideas. You're building foundations for an outlet for your creativity. Revise, rewrite. Missing papers or objects are found.

Sunday, July 22 (Moon in Virgo)   The moon is in your twelfth house today. Unconscious attitudes can be difficult. Keep your feelings secret. You might feel a need to withdraw and work on your own. Take time to reflect and meditate. It's a great time for pursuing a spiritual discipline.

Monday, July 23 (Moon into Libra, 6:39 p.m.)   It's a number 6 day, a service day. Be diplomatic, especially with someone who is giving you trouble. Do a good deed for someone. Visit someone who is ill or in need of help. Be sympathetic, kind, and compassionate, but avoid scattering your energies.

Tuesday, July 24 (Moon in Libra)   The moon is on your ascendant as the month ends. You're recharged for the rest of the month and beyond, and this makes you more appealing to the public. You're physically vital, and relations with the opposite sex go well.

The way you see yourself now is the way others see you. Your thoughts and emotions are aligned.

Wednesday, July 25 (Moon into Scorpio, 10:30 p.m.) It's another power day and your way to play it your way. Open your mind to a new approach that could bring in big bucks. You attract financial success, Libra. Think big and act big! However, you're playing with power, so be careful not to hurt others.

Thursday, July 26 (Moon in Scorpio) The moon is in your second house today, Libra, so it's a good day for dealing with money issues. Pay what you owe, and collect what others owe you. You equate your financial assets with emotional security now. Look at your priorities in handling your income.

Friday, July 27 (Moon in Scorpio) You could experience intense emotions today. You're passionate now, and your sexuality is heightened. Investigate, research, and dig deep for information. Be aware of things happening in secret and of possible deception. Control issues might arise. Best advice: forgive and forget, and try to avoid going to extremes.

Saturday, July 28 (Moon into Sagittarius, 1:18 a.m.) Use your intuition to get a sense of the day. Cooperation is highlighted. Don't make waves. Don't rush or show resentment; let things develop. The spotlight is on cooperation. Show your appreciation to others.

Sunday, July 29 (Moon in Sagittarius) The moon is in your third house today. You have a strong emotional need to get your ideas across. You connect with siblings, and matters from the past are discussed. It's also a good day to write in a journal or study history or archaeology. The past intrigues.

Monday, July 30 (Moon into Capricorn, 3:30 a.m.) It's a number 4 day. Tear down the old in order to rebuild. Be methodical and thorough. Revise, rewrite. Persevere to get things done today. Romance goes onto the back burner for now.

Tuesday, July 31 (Moon in Capricorn) The moon is in your fourth house today, the house of the home. It's a good day to stay home and spend time with your family or work on a home-repair project. You could be dealing with parents now. You feel a close tie to your roots.

AUGUST 2012

Wednesday, August 1 (Moon into Aquarius, 5:56 a.m.) There's a full moon in your fifth house today. That means you get a fresh perspective regarding a love interest. You might be somewhat possessive of loved ones now, particularly children. But eventually you need to let go. It's a good day to take a gamble or buy a lotto ticket. Your emotions tend to overpower your intellect. Your creative energies or romantic inclinations are strong.

Thursday, August 2 (Moon in Aquarius) Your individuality is stressed. At the same time, group activities or social events are highlighted. You have a greater sense of freedom now. You're dealing with new ideas, new options, originality. You get a new perspective. It's a good day to play your hunches and look beyond the immediate.

Friday, August 3 (Moon into Pisces, 9:58 a.m.) It's a number 5 day. That means you're open to change and variety, and you want to loosen any restrictions. You're willing to take a risk and experiment. Variety is the spice of life, and change is good. Think outside the box, Libra.

Saturday, August 4 (Moon in Pisces) With the moon in your sixth house today, the emphasis turns to helping others. Trust your hunches; your intuition is highlighted. Be careful not to overlook any seemingly minor matters that could take on importance. Attend to details related to your health. Make a doctor or dentist appointment that you've been putting off. It's a good day to go to the gym or take a yoga class.

Sunday, August 5 (Moon into Aries, 4:59 p.m.) It's your mystery day, Libra. You venture into the unknown. Secrets, intrigue, confidential information play a role. Be aware of decisions made behind closed doors. You work best on your own today. Gather information, but don't make any absolute decisions until tomorrow.

Monday, August 6 (Moon in Aries) The moon is in your seventh house today. You could be negotiating or signing a contract now, possibly for the sale of property. You're taking the initiative, and emotions could get volatile, especially if you don't inform your partner of everything you're doing. It's difficult to maintain an objective and detached point of view. Keep everyone in balance, Libra, and be careful not to let others manipulate your feelings.

Tuesday, August 7 (Moon in Aries)   Venus moves into your tenth house today. Romance in the workplace, or with someone in a similar career with similar goals, is possible now. You get along well with others, Libra, and your social skills allow you to get ahead in your profession this month.

Wednesday, August 8 (Moon into Taurus, 3:28 a.m.) Mercury goes direct in your eleventh house today. Confusion, miscommunication, and delays, especially related to friends and associates, recede into the past. Things move more smoothly now. You get along with others better, and you get your message across. Everything works better, including computers and other electronic equipment. Others now appreciate all that you do.

Thursday, August 9 (Moon in Taurus)   The moon is in your eighth house today. Take care of any matters related to taxes, insurance, or investments. An inheritance could play a role. Be aware that emotions can get intense now, especially when dealing with shared resources. Metaphysics could play a role in your day. You could be dealing with a mystery of the unknown, such as past lives or what happens after death.

Friday, August 10 (Moon into Gemini, 4:12 p.m.) Your imagination is keen now. You're curious and inventive. Enjoy the harmony, beauty, and pleasures of life. You're warm and receptive to what others say. You have a strong sense of duty and feel obligated to fulfill your promises.

Saturday, August 11 (Moon in Gemini) The moon is in your ninth house today, the home of higher learning. You're considering ideas now on matters such as philosophy or religion, the law or publishing. You also have a strong interest in foreign travel or a foreign nation. Break away from your routine or the usual way you think about things. You can create positive change through your ideas, especially if you express them forcefully.

Sunday, August 12 (Moon in Gemini) It's a good day to take a drive to visit friends or relatives. A change of scenery works well for you now. You also see two sides of an issue today, Libra, so you're in a position to help resolve a dispute. You're feeling creative and need to express yourself in writing or through speech. You're mentally quick and easily get your message across.

Monday, August 13 (Moon into Cancer, 4:29 a.m.) It's a number 6 day, a service day. A domestic adjustment works out for the best. You could face emotional outbursts by someone making unfair demands. Be understanding and avoid confrontations. Help others, but dance to your own tune.

Tuesday, August 14 (Moon in Cancer) The moon is in your tenth house today. Your focus turns to professional matters, whether it's career or education. You could be dealing with a matter related to your reputation, and it works out for the best. You get a boost in prestige now. You're received well by others, but avoid making an emotional display in public.

Wednesday, August 15 (Moon into Leo, 2:06 p.m.) It's another power day, Libra, and you're in the power seat. You can go far with your plans and achieve financial success. You have a chance to expand, to gain recognition even fame and power, especially if you open your mind to a new approach. Remember that you're playing with power, so avoid hurting others.

Thursday, August 16 (Moon in Leo)   The moon is in your eleventh house today. Friends play an important role in your day, especially Gemini and Aquarius. You find strength in numbers and meaning through friends and groups, especially a group of like-minded people working for the common good.

Friday, August 17 (Moon into Virgo, 8:34 p.m.) There's a new moon in your eleventh house today. Focus on your wishes and dreams, Libra. Examine your overall goals; make sure they are still an expression of who you are. You have deeper contact with friends now. It's a good day to join a group of like-minded individuals.

Saturday, August 18 (Moon in Virgo)   With the moon in your twelfth house, there's a tendency to undo all the positive actions you've taken. Avoid any self-destructive behavior. Be aware of hidden enemies. Think carefully before you act today. Best to work on your own and behind the scenes. Take time to reflect and meditate. Unconscious attitudes can be difficult.

Sunday, August 19 (Moon in Virgo)   Stick close to home; focus on tidying up the house. Attend to details and loose ends. You may exhibit some perfectionist tendencies now. Don't forget to exercise and watch your diet. Stop worrying and fretting. Take time to write in a journal or on a blog.

Monday, August 20 (Moon into Libra, 12:46 a.m.) It's a number 4 day. Your organizational skills are highlighted today. Emphasize quality as you fulfill your obligations. Revise and rewrite. You're building foundations for an outlet for your creativity. However, it's not a day for experimentation or new approaches.

Tuesday, August 21 (Moon in Libra)   With the moon on your ascendant today, the way you see yourself is the way others see you. You're feeling physically vital, and your thoughts and emotions are aligned. You're recharged for the month ahead and more appealing to the public. Relations with the opposite sex go well.

Wednesday, August 22 (Moon into Scorpio, 3:54 a.m.)   Domestic purchases are highlighted. Focus on making people happy. Do a good deed. It's a service day, so direct your energy toward helping others. Be generous and tolerant; it goes along with your nature, Libra.

Thursday, August 23 (Moon in Scorpio)   Mars moves into your second house. That means you put more energy into finances over the next three weeks. You have a strong drive to earn money, but an equal willingness to spend it. You're not afraid to take a chance with finances now. However, look at your priorities in handling your income.

Friday, August 24 (Moon into Sagittarius, 6:50 a.m.) Focus on a power play now. Think big and act big! Open your mind to a new approach that could bring in big bucks. You attract financial success. Business discussions go well.

Saturday, August 25 (Moon in Sagittarius)   You're busy keeping your mind occupied with new information. You have a chance to expand whatever you're working on now. You communicate well, but your thinking is unduly influenced by matters from the past. That's especially true in any dealings with siblings, other relatives, or neighbors.

Sunday, August 26 (Moon into Capricorn, 9:59 a.m.) Get out and meet new people, have new experiences, do something you've never done before. Express your opinions dynamically. Explore and discover. Creativity is highlighted. In romance, a flirtation could turn more serious now.

Monday, August 27 (Moon in Capricorn)   The moon is in your fourth house today. Try to spend more time at home with loved ones now. Beautify your surroundings with a home-repair or redecoration project.

Show that you care. You feel a close tie to your roots. It's a good day to retreat to a private place for meditation and put everything into perspective.

Tuesday, August 28 (Moon into Aquarius, 1:39 p.m.) Take time to relax, enjoy yourself, and recharge your batteries. You can influence people now with your upbeat attitude. Your charm and wit are appreciated. Foster generosity. In romance, you're an ardent and loyal lover.

Wednesday, August 29 (Moon in Aquarius) The moon is in your fifth house today. Be yourself; be emotionally honest. Follow your heart on a creative project. You can tap deeply into the collective unconscious for inspiration. In romance, make an effort to avoid being overly possessive.

Thursday, August 30 (Moon into Pisces, 6:32 p.m.) Variety is the spice of life now. Think outside the box. Take risks, experiment; get a new point of view. Follow your curiosity. However, don't spread yourself too thin.

Friday, August 31 (Moon in Pisces) Mercury moves into your twelfth house today. It's a good time for meditation or therapy or any mind-body discipline. It's also a good time for working behind the scenes, especially on a writing project. You have ready access to your dreams. There's also a full moon in your sixth house, so you can gain a better understanding of a health matter.

Saturday, September 1 (Moon in Pisces) The moon is in your sixth house today. It's a service day. Others rely on you for help now. You're the one they go to for help, especially family members. You improve, edit, and refine the work of others. Offer help, but don't deny your own needs. Take care of any health-care issues.

Sunday, September 2 (Moon into Aries, 1:38 a.m.) It's a number 5 day. Freedom and change are highlighted now. Variety is the spice of life. Think outside the box. Take risks, experiment. Let go of old structures; get a new point of view, a new perspective on things.

Monday, September 3 (Moon in Aries) The moon is in your seventh house today. Partnerships are highlighted. You get along well with others and feel more secure when everyone is in agreement with you. You can fit in just about anywhere. It's best not to make waves right now.

Tuesday, September 4 (Moon into Taurus, 11:42 a.m.) It's your mystery day, Libra. Best to work on your own. Secrets, intrigue, confidential information play a role. You investigate, analyze, or simply observe what's going on now. You quickly come to a conclusion and wonder why others don't see what you see. You detect deception and recognize insincerity with ease. Maintain your emotional balance.

Wednesday, September 5 (Moon in Taurus)   The moon is in your eighth house today. If you are planning on making a major purchase, make sure that you and your partner are in agreement. Otherwise, you could encounter intense emotional resistance. An interest in metaphysics plays a role in your day. You could be dealing with a mystery of the unknown.

Thursday, September 6 (Moon in Taurus)   With Venus moving into your eleventh house today, you can gain financially or professionally through the help of friends this month. You work very well with colleagues and friends, especially in a group, and have a knack for putting others at ease. It's also a good time for exploring your artistic talents.

Friday, September 7 (Moon into Gemini, 12:11 a.m.)   It's a number 1 day, and you're at the top of your cycle. Trust your hunches; intuition is highlighted. Don't be afraid to turn in a new direction. You're inventive and make connections that others overlook. You're determined and courageous today. In romance, make room for a new love, if that's what you want.

Saturday, September 8 (Moon in Gemini)   The moon is in your ninth house today. You yearn for a new experience. Plan a long trip. Sign up for a workshop or seminar. Foreigners or a foreign country plays a role. Your mind is active and you're interested in ideas, mythology, philosophy, or religion. You can create positive change through your ideas.

Sunday, September 9 (Moon into Cancer, 12:50 p.m.)
Your attitude determines everything today. You communicate well. You're warm and receptive to what others say. Don't forget to spread your own good news. Your charm and wit are appreciated.

Monday, September 10 (Moon in Cancer) The moon is in your tenth house today. You focus on career or professional matters now. You're dealing with your reputation, your need for recognition. You deal well with the public now and are responsive to the needs of coworkers and the public at large.

Tuesday, September 11 (Moon into Leo, 11:01 p.m.)
Promote new ideas; follow your curiosity. Think outside the box today. It's a good day to take a risk or experiment. You're versatile and changeable, Libra. But be careful not to spread out and diversify too much.

Wednesday, September 12 (Moon in Leo) The moon is in your eleventh house today. You have deeper contact with friends now. You find strength in numbers. You find meaning through friends and groups. You work for the common good. Aquarius or Gemini plays a role in your day.

Thursday, September 13 (Moon in Leo) Strut your stuff today, Libra! Be wild and imaginative; be the person you always imagined you might be. Play with different personae. Theatrics and drama are highlighted. You're creative and passionate today, impulsive and honest.

Friday, September 14 (Moon into Virgo, 5:31 a.m.)
It's your power day and your day to play it your way.
Unexpected money arrives. You pull off a financial
coup. Business discussions go well. It's a good day for
buying a lottery ticket. Financial gain is at hand.

Saturday, September 15 (Moon in Virgo)   There's
a new moon in your twelfth house today. It's a good
day to stay out of sight and work behind the scenes.
You find new opportunities now, but it's best to keep
them to yourself for the time being. Take time to reflect and meditate. Pay attention to synchronicities
and see where they lead you.

Sunday, September 16 (Moon into Libra, 8:55 a.m.)
With Mercury moving into your first house today,
you're mentally restless. You enjoy conversing and
making connections, not necessary to attract new
friends, but to learn something new. You easily adapt
to changing situations and express yourself well.
You're searching for ways to improve yourself.

Monday, September 17 (Moon in Libra)   Pluto
goes direct in your fourth house today. Underlying
power struggles in your home environment could
start to surface, or such struggles could develop. You
feel strongly attached to your home or the land you
think of as your own. There's a tendency to feel that
you need to dominate a domestic situation and make
sure others know your position.

*Tuesday, September 18 (Moon into Scorpio, 10:46
a.m.)*   Things take a lighter turn today. Your atti-

tude determines everything. Ease up on routines. Spread your good news, and take time to listen to others. Your charm and wit are appreciated, Libra.

Wednesday, September 19 (Moon in Scorpio) With the moon in your second house, you're feeling a sense of abundance. You expand your horizons with a new purchase, or new money arrives. You're in a fortunate position, but don't overextend yourself. Look at your priorities in handling your income.

Thursday, September 20 (Moon into Sagittarius, 12:34 p.m.) Approach the day with an unconventional mind-set. Promote new ideas; follow your curiosity. Look for adventure. Freedom of thought and action is key. But so is moderation; avoid excess in whatever you're doing. You're courageous and adaptable.

Friday, September 21 (Moon in Sagittarius) With the moon in your third house today, it's a good time for expressing yourself through writing. Take what you know and share it with others. As you go about your everyday life, look to the past for clues about what's coming up in the near future. Expect an invitation to a social event.

Saturday, September 22 (Moon into Capricorn, 3:21 p.m.) It's another mystery day. You launch a journey into the unknown. Secrets, intrigue, confidential information play a role. Make sure that you see things as they are, not as you wish them to be. Express your desires, but avoid self-deception. Maintain your emotional balance, Libra.

Sunday, September 23 (Moon in Capricorn) The moon is in your fourth house today. You're dealing with the foundations of who you are and who you are becoming. A parent plays a role in your day. Retreat to a private place for meditation. It's a good day for dream recall or changing a bad habit.

Monday, September 24 (Moon into Aquarius, 7:33 p.m.) Finish whatever you've been working on. Look for a new approach, a new perspective. The old cycle is ending; a new one about to begin. Visualize the future; set your goals, then make them so.

Tuesday, September 25 (Moon in Aquarius) The moon is in your fifth house today. You can move ahead on any creative project. Meanwhile, you have an opportunity to achieve greater depth in a relationship, but it could take hard work. Be yourself; be emotionally honest.

Wednesday, September 26 (Moon in Aquarius) Groups and social events are highlighted today. You're dealing with new ideas, new options, originality. Bust old paradigms. You get a new perspective. Help others, but dance to your own tune. Your wishes and dreams come true.

Thursday, September 27 (Moon into Pisces, 1:25 a.m.) You're creative and express yourself well today. Your artistic talents and imagination are highlighted. You can tap deeply into the collective unconscious for inspiration. Enjoy the harmony, beauty, and pleasures of life.

Friday, September 28 (Moon in Pisces)   The moon is in your sixth house today. Delegate some of your responsibilities; avoid taking on too much work. You help others, but allow them to shoulder some of the burden. Don't become a martyr for someone else's cause. Take care of any health issues.

Saturday, September 29 (Moon into Aries, 9:15 a.m.) There's a full moon in your seventh house today. You gain insight related to a marriage or partnership. A contract could be involved. You reap what you've sown; it's a time of completion.

Sunday, September 30 (Moon in Aries)   It's a great time for initiating projects, launching new ideas, brainstorming. You can be very persuasive now. You're passionate but impatient. It's also a good day to attend a sports event. Wear bright colors. Imprint your style. Look for excitement and adventure.

OCTOBER 2012

Monday, October 1 (Moon into Taurus, 7:27 p.m.) Travel and variety are highlighted today. You're versatile, changeable. Be careful not to spread out and diversify too much. Freedom of thought and action is key. But so is moderation; avoid excess in whatever you're doing. A change of scenery would work to your advantage.

Tuesday, October 2 (Moon in Taurus)   The moon in your eighth house can affect your feelings about your possessions, as well as things that you share with others, such as a spouse. You have a strong sense of duty and feel obligated to fulfill your promises. Security is an important issue with you right now.

Wednesday, October 3 (Moon in Taurus)   Venus moves into your twelfth house today. You have a love of solitude. You enjoy working on your own or behind the scenes. You're not telling everyone something that you know. You tend to keep your emotions under control now.

Thursday, October 4 (Moon into Gemini, 7:47 a.m.) It's a number 8 day, your power day. Business discussions go well. You attract financial success. Open your mind to a new approach that could bring in big bucks. You have a chance to expand, to gain recognition, even fame and power.

Friday, October 5 (Moon in Gemini)   With Mercury moving into your second house today, you could be dealing with some changes in your finances. There's lots of talk about money issues. Meanwhile, Saturn joins Mercury in your second house, where it will stay for two and a half years. That means you have better structure and stability in your finances over the next couple of years. However, there could be some setbacks and delays, especially if you try a get-rich-quick scheme. Romance now could involve someone who deals with money matters.

Saturday, October 6 (Moon into Cancer, 8:46 p.m.) Mars moves into your third house today. That means there's strong energy for the rest of the month related to whatever you're doing in your everyday world. You're busy keeping your mind occupied with new information, and now you see the big picture. However, try not to get impatient with people who aren't up to your speed and energy level. Keep conscious control of your emotions when communicating, especially with siblings or neighbors.

Sunday, October 7 (Moon in Cancer)   It's a good day to stick close to home and spend time with family members. You're intuitive and nurturing, and your home life is important to you. Do something with your children, other loved ones, or sweetheart. It's also a good day to beautify your home or take care of some necessary repairs.

Monday, October 8 (Moon in Cancer)   With the moon in your tenth house today, there's lots of activity now in your professional life. You love what you do and communicate well. You feel very emotional about your work or your fellow workers. You're in the public eye and gain a boost in prestige.

Tuesday, October 9 (Moon into Leo, 7:55 a.m.) It's a number 4 day, and it's time to get focused. Persevere to get things done today, and don't get sloppy. Tear down the old in order to rebuild. Be methodical and thorough, and stay on task. Revise and rewrite.

Wednesday, October 10 (Moon in Leo)   The moon is in your eleventh house today. Friends play an important role in your day. You find strength in numbers and meaning through friends and groups. Focus on your wishes and dreams. Examine your overall goals. Those goals should be an expression of who you are.

Thursday, October 11 (Moon into Virgo, 3:24 p.m.)
A domestic adjustment works out for the best. Don't let it go any longer; it won't get better. You could face emotional outbursts or someone making unfair demands. Be diplomatic and understanding. Service to others is the theme of the day.

Friday, October 12 (Moon in Virgo)   The moon is in your twelfth house today. Think carefully before you act. There's a tendency now to undo all the positive actions you've taken. Avoid any self-destructive behavior. Be aware of hidden enemies. You might feel a need to withdraw and work on your own. Things associated with the past and your childhood play a role.

Saturday, October 13 (Moon into Libra, 7:02 p.m.)
It's another power day and your day to play it your way. You can go far with your plans and achieve financial success. You have a chance to expand, to gain recognition, even fame. Business discussions go well. You pull off a financial coup.

Sunday, October 14 (Moon in Libra)   With the moon in your first house today, your feelings and thoughts are aligned. It's all about your health and your emotional self: how you feel and how you feel about yourself. You're sensitive and responsive to the needs of others, so you can be easily influenced by those around you.

Monday, October 15 (Moon into Scorpio, 8:07 p.m.)
There's a new moon in your first house, Libra. New
personal opportunities come your way. It's all about
the way you see yourself and how you relate to a romantic partner. Intuition is highlighted. You have an
opportunity to expand your life with that special person. Romance is emphasized.

Tuesday, October 16 (Moon in Scorpio)   The
moon is in your second house today. You tend to react
emotionally now to an event in your life related to
money or your values. You identify emotionally with
your possessions or whatever you value. Look at your
priorities in handling your income; watch your spending.

*Wednesday, October 17 (Moon into Sagittarius, 8:26
p.m.)*   It's a number 3 day. That means your imagination is keen now, and you communicate well.
You're curious and inventive. You're warm and receptive to what others say. Enjoy the harmony, beauty,
and pleasures of life. You have a strong sense of duty
and feel obligated to fulfill your promises.

Thursday, October 18 (Moon in Sagittarius)   The
moon is in your third house today. You tend to move
about, going from one place to another or one project
to another. You're moving ahead, but your thoughts
are focused on a matter from the past. An interest in
history or archaeology is highlighted.

Friday, October 19 (Moon into Capricorn, 9:42 p.m.)
You're motivated and inspired. It's a good time to pur-

sue self-employment. You're courageous and adaptable. A change of scenery would work to your advantage. You could be moving to a new location.

Saturday, October 20 (Moon in Capricorn)   With the moon in your fourth house, you feel a close tie to your roots today. You could be dealing with parents. You're dealing with the foundations of who you are and who you are becoming. It's a good day for dream recall. Retreat to a private place for meditation.

Sunday, October 21 (Moon in Capricorn)   Elderly people or authority figures play a role in your day. Maintain emotional balance. Set your goals, then make them so. Be conservative with your money; don't speculate or take any unnecessary risks.

Monday, October 22 (Moon into Aquarius, 1:03 a.m.)   It's your power day, your day to play it your way. Business discussions work in your favor now. You could pull off a financial coup. Financial gain is at hand. Unexpected money arrives. It's a good day for buying a lottery ticket.

Tuesday, October 23 (Moon in Aquarius)   With the moon in your fifth house today, you're feeling a sudden surge of inspiration, a creative urge that helps you break through a block. In romance, there's more depth and understanding in a relationship. Children play an important role in your day.

Wednesday, October 24 (Moon into Pisces, 7:01 a.m.)   It's a number 1 day, and you're at the top of your cycle. You take the lead in something new and get a fresh start, a new beginning. Stress originality. You attract creative people and avoid people with closed minds. Trust your hunches.

Thursday, October 25 (Moon in Pisces)   The moon is in your sixth house today. Your personal health occupies your attention. Keep your resolutions about exercise, and watch your diet. Attend to details related to your health. Make a doctor or dentist appointment, if needed. Help others, but don't deny your own needs.

Friday, October 26 (Moon into Aries, 3:32 p.m.) Remain flexible in your schedule today. Make time to listen to others. Your charm and wit are appreciated. Spread your good news; you communicate well. Take time to relax, enjoy yourself, and recharge your batteries.

Saturday, October 27 (Moon in Aries)   The moon is in your seventh house today. Loved ones and partners are more important than usual. You get along well with others now. Women play a prominent role. You can fit in just about anywhere. However, you might have trouble getting in touch with your own feelings.

Sunday, October 28 (Moon in Aries)   With Venus moving into your first house today, you're more socially outgoing than usual. Others appreciate your personal grace and friendly attitude. Your outlook on life becomes more upbeat over the next three weeks.

You develop new friendships. You like the way you look now, but avoid becoming vain about it.

Monday, October 29 (Moon into Taurus, 2:16 a.m.)
With Mercury moving into your second house today, Libra, yesterday's energy flows into your Monday. You can come up with some money-making ideas over the next three weeks. Your quick-thinking ability is put to use for financial affairs now, and you can easily communicate those ideas so they can be put into place. Your values deal primarily with material success. The full moon in Taurus adds to your sense of abundance. You reap what you have sown.

Tuesday, October 30 (Moon in Taurus) The moon is in your eighth house today. You can expect heightened emotions regarding a troubling matter, especially if it deals with shared belongings. You dig deep, seeking more details. A mortgage, insurance, or investments could play a role. Maintain your emotional and mental balance, and avoid any tendencies toward greed or possessiveness. Meanwhile, you could be looking into a metaphysical subject, such as life after death or astrology.

Wednesday, October 31 (Moon into Gemini, 2:41 p.m.) You end the month on another power day, so it's time to make a power play. You have a chance to expand, to gain recognition, even fame and power. You attract financial success. You're being watched by people in power.

Thursday, November 1 (Moon in Gemini)   The moon is in your ninth house today. You're a dreamer and a thinker. You may feel a need to get away now, a break from the usual routine. You yearn for a new experience. Plan a long trip. Sign up for a workshop or seminar.

Friday, November 2 (Moon in Gemini)   You're feeling restless today and sending text messages to friends and associates to pass the time. Your mind moves quickly from one thought to another. Write, revise, and publicize. You see two sides of an issue, Libra. You're a good mediator now. You keep everyone around you in balance.

Saturday, November 3 (Moon into Cancer, 3:43 a.m.)   It's your power day, and you can play it your way. You're in the power seat. You have a chance to expand, to gain recognition, fame, power. You attract financial success, especially if you open your mind to a new approach.

Sunday, November 4—Daylight Saving Time Ends (Moon in Cancer)   With the moon in your tenth house today, you're concerned about your career or profession. You're looking for a promotion, a raise, or a boost in prestige. You could be talking with fellow workers, but it's best to keep your professional and private lives separate.

Monday, November 5 (Moon into Leo, 3:40 p.m.) You're at the top of your cycle again. You're inventive and make connections that others overlook. You're determined and courageous today. Stress originality in whatever you're doing, and don't be afraid to turn in a new direction. Express your opinions dynamically.

Tuesday, November 6 (Moon in Leo)   Mercury goes retrograde in your third house and stays retrograde until November 26. Watch out for miscommunication or misunderstanding with family members, especially siblings, and neighbors over the next three weeks. Leave enough time for delays in your everyday travel. There could be confusion about matters related to past events.

Wednesday, November 7 (Moon in Leo)   The moon is in your eleventh house today, Libra. You work well with others, especially in a group. Friends play a surprisingly important role, especially Gemini and Libra. Focus on your wishes and dreams. Examine your overall goals, and make sure that they're still an expression of who you are.

Thursday, November 8 (Moon into Virgo, 12:36 a.m.)   Your organizational skills are highlighted now, but try not to wander off task. Emphasize quality; you're building a creative foundation for your future. Tear down the old in order to rebuild. Be methodical and thorough.

Friday, November 9 (Moon in Virgo)   The moon is in your twelfth house today. You might feel a need to withdraw and work on your own. Think carefully before you act. There's a tendency now to undo all the positive actions you've taken. Avoid any self-destructive behavior. Be aware of hidden enemies.

Saturday, November 10 (Moon into Libra, 5:36 a.m.)   Neptune goes direct in your sixth house today. You feel a strong compulsion to help others. Service is a spiritual task for you. You might have glamorous illusions about such work. You also have difficulty concentrating on mundane jobs and attending to details. Routine work can be a continuing problem.

Sunday, November 11 (Moon in Libra)   The moon is on your ascendant today. The way you see yourself now is the way others see you. Your appearance and personality shine. You're physically vital, and relations with the opposite sex go well.

Monday, November 12 (Moon into Scorpio, 7:11 a.m.)   It's another power day, and you're on top of your game. You can go far with your plans, especially if you open your mind to a new approach. You're being watched by people in power. Be courageous. Be yourself; be honest.

Tuesday, November 13 (Moon in Scorpio)   There's a solar eclipse in your second house today. That means new financial opportunities come your way. This is considered a very positive eclipse. Jupiter is also forming a positive angle that should allow you to expand whatever you're doing.

Wednesday, November 14 (Moon into Sagittarius, 6:53 a.m.)   Mercury now retrogrades back to Scorpio, your second house, where it will stay until November 26. Watch out for miscommunication or misunderstanding related to money matters. The big opportunities that came your way yesterday might not be understood by someone close to you. You're excited, but the other person is wary, causing confusion. Watch your spending over the next couple of weeks. Put off any major purchases until the end of the month.

Thursday, November 15 (Moon in Sagittarius) The moon is in your third house today. You write from a deep place. It's a good day for journaling. Be aware that your thinking may be unduly influenced by things from the past. You could be visiting with relatives or siblings or spending time in the community with your neighbors. You accept an invitation to a social event.

Friday, November 16 (Moon into Capricorn, 6:36 a.m.)   Mars moves into your fourth house today. You put a lot of energy into your home life now. That could mean some major renovations. You could encounter some disagreements and quarreling within the family or a time of activism related to the environment.

Saturday, November 17 (Moon in Capricorn) With the moon in your fourth house today, yesterday's energy flows into your Saturday. You're dealing with the foundations of who you are and who you are becoming. Spend time with your family and loved ones. Stick close to home. A parent plays a role in your day.

Sunday, November 18 (Moon into Aquarius, 8:11 a.m.)   You're seeking new horizons. Release old structures; get a new point of view. Think outside the box. Variety is the spice of life. Freedom of thought and action is key. You can easily overcome obstacles today.

Monday, November 19 (Moon in Aquarius)   The moon is in your fifth house today, Libra. Be yourself; be emotionally honest. In love, there's greater emotional depth to a relationship now. You might be somewhat possessive of loved ones now, particularly children. But eventually you need to let go.

Tuesday, November 20 (Moon into Pisces, 12:55 p.m.)   You launch a journey into the unknown and pursue a mystery. Dig deep and look behind closed doors. Confidential information and secrets are involved. But don't make any final decisions on what you uncover until tomorrow.

Wednesday, November 21 (Moon in Pisces)   Venus moves into your second house today. You have a love of personal adornments now, whether that means jewelry, clothing, or even an upgrade in the vehicle you're driving. Wealth, whether you have it or are aspiring to it, makes you feel good. You can make money with your artistic abilities, and that's especially true over the next three weeks.

Thursday, November 22 (Moon into Aries, 9:12 p.m.)   It's a number 9 day. That means it's a good time to finish what you started. Visualize the future;

set your goals, then make them so. Look beyond the immediate. Get ready for something new. Strive for universal appeal.

Friday, November 23 (Moon in Aries)   The moon is in your seventh house today. Loved ones and partners are more important than usual. You get along well with others now. You can fit in just about anywhere. You feel a need to be accepted. You're looking for security, but you have a hard time going with the flow.

Saturday, November 24 (Moon in Aries)   Take time to relax, enjoy yourself, recharge your batteries. You can influence people now with your upbeat attitude. Your charm and wit are appreciated. Foster generosity. In romance, you're an ardent and loyal lover.

Sunday, November 25 (Moon into Taurus, 8:18 a.m.) Take time to relax on this Sunday. Enjoy yourself; recharge your batteries. You can influence people now with your upbeat attitude. Your charm and wit are appreciated. Foster generosity. In romance, you're an ardent and loyal lover.

Monday, November 26 (Moon in Taurus)   Mercury goes direct in your second house today. Any confusion or miscommunication that you've been experiencing, especially related to finances, recedes into the past. Things move more smoothly now. You get your ideas across. Others understand your values or what you value.

Tuesday, November 27 (Moon into Gemini, 8:59 p.m.)   You're versatile and changeable now. However, be careful not to spread out and diversify too much. Get a new point of view; follow your curiosity. Freedom of thought and action is key. But so is moderation; avoid excess in whatever you're doing.

Wednesday, November 28 (Moon in Gemini) There's a lunar eclipse in your ninth house today. You react emotionally to a matter related to long-distance travel or higher education. You could be preparing for a long romantic journey now. You could also develop a strong attachment to a foreign-born person or a foreign land.

Thursday, November 29 (Moon in Gemini)   You're restless and busy, getting in touch with friends and associates with phone calls, e-mails, or text messages. You're mentally quick and communicate well. You get your message across. It's a good time to socialize, maybe visit a bookstore with friends or go out to lunch.

Friday, November 30 (Moon into Cancer, 9:56 a.m.) The month ends on a power day. You can go far with your plans and achieve financial success. That's especially true if you act with courage and conviction. Be aware that fear of failure or fear that you won't measure up will attract tangible experiences that reinforce the feeling.

DECEMBER 2012

Saturday, December 1 (Moon in Cancer)   The moon is in your tenth house today. Career matters are on your mind. You're looking for an advancement, a raise, or a boost in prestige. You're more responsive to the needs and moods of a group and of the public in general. You're more open and accessible now, but take care to avoid emotional displays, especially in public.

Sunday, December 2 (Moon into Leo, 9:58 p.m.) It's another power day, Libra; you're in the power seat. Think big and act big! However, be aware that you're playing with power so try not to hurt anyone. Open your mind to a new approach that could bring in big bucks.

Monday, December 3 (Moon in Leo)   The moon is in your eleventh house today. Friends play an important role in your day. You find strength in numbers and meaning through friends and groups. Focus on your wishes and dreams. Examine your overall goals. Those goals should be an expression of who you are.

Tuesday, December 4 (Moon in Leo)   Drama is highlighted, perhaps involving children. You like to flaunt and celebrate now. Be wild and imaginative, Libra. Bring out your inner child. Be the person you always imagined you might be. Play with different personae. You're creative and passionate today, impulsive and honest.

Wednesday, December 5 (Moon into Virgo, 7:53 a.m.) Use your intuition to get a sense of your day. Don't make waves. Don't rush or show resentment; let things develop. You excel in working with others. You're playing the role of the visionary today.

Thursday, December 6 (Moon in Virgo) The moon is in your twelfth house today. It's best to stay out of public view for now. Difficult issues from your past might surface. Confide your thoughts and feelings to a close friend or confidante. Relations with women can be difficult.

Friday, December 7 (Moon into Libra, 2:37 p.m.) Your organizational skills are highlighted today. Clean out your garage, the attic, or a closet. Organize your files. Get rid of what you no longer need. Tear down the old in order to rebuild. Missing papers are found. Be practical with your money.

Saturday, December 8 (Moon in Libra) You're sensitive to the moods of others now, and you try to keep everyone around you in balance. You're good at developing friendships and making contact with old friends. The way you see yourself is the way others see you. You feel recharged for the month ahead, and this makes you more appealing to the public. Relations with the opposite sex go well.

Sunday, December 9 (Moon into Scorpio, 5:52 p.m.) Service to others is the theme of the day. You offer advice and support. Be sympathetic and kind, generous and tolerant. Focus on making people happy on this Sunday. However, avoid scattering your energies.

Monday, December 10 (Moon in Scorpio) Mercury moves into your third house today. There's a lot to communicate now as the work week begins. You get your ideas across as you go about your business, but it's more of an intellectual pursuit than an emotional one. You're witty, alert, and adaptable. Think of ways to expand whatever you're doing.

Tuesday, December 11 (Moon into Sagittarius, 6:22 p.m.) It's another power day, Libra. That means it's your day to play it your way. Now you can go far with your plans and achieve financial success. Expect a windfall. However, be aware that you're playing with power, so try not to hurt anyone.

Wednesday, December 12 (Moon in Sagittarius) The focus of your activities is more mental than physical now, Libra. You communicate your thoughts and ideas well. You see the big picture, not just the details. But make sure you control your emotions. Avoid arguments, especially with siblings and other relatives. You could receive an invitation to a social event.

Thursday, December 13 (Moon into Capricorn, 5:43 p.m.) There's a new moon in your third house, indicating that you find new opportunities in your everyday life. It's a good day to take a gamble. With Uranus going direct in your seventh house today, you could be involved in a marriage or partnership that is somewhat unconventional. Your ideas about a partnership become more unusual over time. You're looking for more independence, and as a result you tend to behave erratically in a partnership or marriage.

Friday, December 14 (Moon in Capricorn)   You're dealing with the foundations of who you are and who you are becoming. Retreat to a private place for meditation. It's a good day for dream recall. It's best to work on your own and stay focused. It's time to eliminate a bad habit.

Saturday, December 15 (Moon into Aquarius, 5:53 p.m.)   Venus moves into your third house today. You get along well with family members this month, especially siblings. You could be getting involved with neighbors in a community project that you really enjoy. You're more artistic in your outlook.

Sunday, December 16 (Moon in Aquarius)   The moon is in your fifth house today. Your creativity, personal grace, and magnetism are highlighted. It's a good day to pursue a creative project. Animals play a larger role. You're also more protective and nurturing toward any children in your life.

Monday, December 17 (Moon into Pisces, 8:48 p.m.) It's a number 5 day. That means travel and variety are highlighted. You're seeking new horizons. Promote new ideas; follow your curiosity. Look for adventure. You're versatile and changeable. Be careful not to spread out and diversify too much.

Tuesday, December 18 (Moon in Pisces) The moon is in your sixth house today. You enjoy your work now and get along with fellow workers. The work environment is harmonious, and you keep everyone in balance, Libra. Be careful not to overlook any seemingly minor matters that could take on importance. Keep up with your exercise plan, and watch your diet.

Wednesday, December 19 (Moon in Pisces) You can tap deeply into the collective unconscious for inspiration. It's a time of deep healing. Watch for psychic events, synchronicities. Keep track of your dreams, including your daydreams. Ideas are ripe. Imagination is highlighted.

Thursday, December 20 (Moon into Aries, 3:44 a.m.) It's your power day, Libra. Time for a power play. Business dealings go well, especially if you open your mind to a new approach. Expect a windfall. You're being watched by people in power. Be courageous. Be yourself; be honest.

Friday, December 21 (Moon in Aries) The moon is in your seventh house today. You communicate well with a spouse or partner. It's all about working together. A contract or a lawsuit could play a role. You get along well with others, but it's a challenge to remain detached and objective.

Saturday, December 22 (Moon into Taurus, 2:26 p.m.) It's a number 1 day, and you're at the top of your cycle on this Saturday. You get a fresh start, a new beginning. Trust your hunches; intuition is highlighted. Get out and meet new people and have new experiences. Do something you've never done before.

Sunday, December 23 (Moon in Taurus) With the moon in your eighth house today, your experiences are more intense than usual. Managing shared resources takes on new importance. It's a good day for dealing with mortgages, insurance, and investments. Other issues of the day could include matters of sex, death, rebirth, rituals, and relationships. An interest in metaphysics plays a role.

Monday, December 24 (Moon in Taurus) It's a good day to use common sense and take a down-to-earth perspective on whatever you're doing. Cultivate new ideas, but try to avoid stubborn behavior when others question your actions. You could be somewhat possessive now.

Tuesday, December 25 (Moon into Gemini, 3:14 a.m.) With Mars moving into your fifth house today, you're energetic and actively pursuing the pleasures and joys of life. Romance is highlighted and so are your creative talents. Avoid any petty jealousies. It's a good day to take a chance. Merry Christmas!

Wednesday, December 26 (Moon in Gemini) The moon is in your ninth house today. If you're feeling somewhat stressed and overworked, relax and take a deep breath. Plans for travel or higher education play a role. Sign up for a seminar or workshop. Study a foreign destination you want to visit or take a lesson in another language. A person of foreign birth could play a role.

Thursday, December 27 (Moon into Cancer, 4:08 p.m.)   Diplomacy wins the way. Focus on making people happy. Do a good deed. Be sympathetic and kind, generous and tolerant. But know when enough is enough. Avoid scattering your energies.

Friday, December 28 (Moon in Cancer)   There's a full moon in your tenth house today. A new opportunity to move ahead in your career comes your way, possibly an advancement, a raise, or a new project. You get along well with fellow workers, but be careful not to mix your personal and professional lives now.

Saturday, December 29 (Moon in Cancer)   Your home and family life are emphasized today. Tend to loved ones; do something with your children or sweetheart. You could be somewhat moody. Best to keep your thoughts to yourself. Don't criticize, condemn, or complain.

Sunday, December 30 (Moon into Leo, 3:47 a.m.) It's a number 9 day and a good day to clear your desk and make room for the new, but don't start anything new until tomorrow. Spend some time in deep thought. Spiritual values arise. Use the day for reflection, expansion, and concluding projects. Strive for universal appeal.

Monday, December 31 (Moon in Leo)   With Mercury moving into your fourth house today, you communicate well, especially with family members about domestic matters. You spread your ideas, especially those about a home-repair project. Things move smoothly, and others understand what you want.

HAPPY NEW YEAR!

JANUARY 2013

Tuesday, January 1 (Moon into Virgo, 12:36 p.m.) Service to others is the rule of the day and a guiding theme for the year! Adjust to the needs of loved ones. A change in the home is needed now. Don't put off the situation; that will only aggravate the problem. You can keep everyone around you in balance, Libra.

Wednesday, January 2 (Moon in Virgo) The moon is in your twelfth house today. Think carefully before you act. Unconscious attitudes can be difficult. There's a tendency now to undo all the positive actions you've taken. Avoid any self-destructive behavior. Be aware of hidden enemies. Take time to reflect and meditate.

Thursday, January 3 (Moon into Libra, 8:12 p.m.) It's your power day, your day to play it your way. More money comes your way from a financial venture. Think big and act big! Unexpected resources arrive. It's a good day to buy a lotto ticket.

Friday, January 4 (Moon in Libra) The moon is on your ascendant today. The way you see yourself now is the way others see you. You're feeling recharged and ready to go. You're physically vital, and relations with the opposite sex go well. Your appearance and personality shine.

Saturday, January 5 (Moon in Libra)   The moon is in your first house today. Spread your wings and fly. Don't limit yourself. You could easily change your mind now about an important matter. You're restless and uncertain what to do. You are sensitive and responsive regarding the needs of others, so you are easily influenced by those around you.

Sunday, January 6 (Moon into Scorpio, 1:10 a.m.) It's a number 2 day. Use your intuition to get a sense of your day. Be kind and understanding. Cooperation, especially with partners, is highlighted. Don't make waves. Don't rush or show resentment; let things develop. Marriage plays a key role.

Monday, January 7 (Moon in Scorpio)   The moon is in your second house today. It's a good day to expand your money-making possibilities, Libra. What's the big picture in financial terms? Your values are important to you in determining how to proceed.

Tuesday, January 8 (Moon into Sagittarius, 3:29 a.m.) It's a number 4 day. Keep your goals in mind; follow your ideas. Be tenacious. You tend to stay with the tried and true. It's not a day for experimentation or new approaches. Take care of your obligations. You're building foundations for an outlet for your creativity. Emphasize quality.

Wednesday, January 9 (Moon in Sagittarius) Venus moves into your fourth house. There's harmony in
the home this month. Spend time with your family
and other loved ones. Stick close to home. You're
dealing with the foundations of who you are and who
you are becoming. Take time to retreat to a private
place for meditation. It's a good time for dream recall.

***Thursday, January 10 (Moon into Capricorn, 3:55
a.m.)*** A change in the home, an adjustment or readjustment, is needed now. Don't put off the situation;
that will only aggravate the problem. Offer advice and
support. Be sympathetic and kind, generous and tolerant. Try to avoid confrontations.

Friday, January 11 (Moon in Capricorn) With a
new moon in your fourth house, new opportunities
come your way related to your home life. That could
mean it's a good time to start a new domestic project,
especially if you have a home-based business, or you
could get a chance to move ahead on a project to renovate, repair, or beautify your house.

***Saturday, January 12 (Moon into Aquarius, 4:02
a.m.)*** It's a number 6 day, a service day. Be diplomatic, especially with someone who is giving you
trouble. Do a good deed for someone. Visit someone
who is ill or in need of help. Be sympathetic, kind, and
compassionate, but avoid scattering your energies.

Sunday, January 13 (Moon in Aquarius) The
moon is in your fifth house today. Romance and sex
for pleasure are highlighted. Your emotions tend to

overpower your intellect now, and you're emotionally in touch with your creative side. You feel strongly attached to loved ones, particularly children.

Monday, January 14 (Moon into Pisces, 5:50 a.m.)
It's a number 1 day, and you're at the top of your cycle. Be independent and creative, and refuse to be discouraged by naysayers. Take the lead, get a fresh start, a new beginning, and don't be afraid to turn in a new direction. Trust your hunches.

Tuesday, January 15 (Moon in Pisces)   The moon is in your sixth house today. It's a good day to clarify any health or work issues. It's best if you follow a regular schedule now. Help others where you can, but don't deny your own needs.

Wednesday, January 16 (Moon into Aries, 11:08 a.m.)   You're creative and express yourself well today. Your artistic talents are highlighted, Libra. It's your kind of day. Enjoy the harmony, beauty, and pleasures of life. Remember to remain flexible.

Thursday, January 17 (Moon in Aries)   With the moon in your seventh house today, partnerships are explored in a new venture or adventure. Loved ones and partners are more important than usual. You get along well with others. You can fit in just about anywhere.

Friday, January 18 (Moon into Taurus, 8:37 p.m.)
Variety is the spice of life. You're seeking new horizons. Think outside the box; it's a good day to take

risks or experiment. You're versatile and changeable. Release old structures; get a new point of view.

Saturday, January 19 (Moon in Taurus) With Mercury moving into your fifth house today, there's lots of discussion about your artistic and creative talents. You speak and write well now. You're also very analytical this month, easily dissecting matters that interest you, including romance.

Sunday, January 20 (Moon in Taurus) With the moon in your eighth house today, you take an interest in a spiritual or metaphysical subject. You dig deep for information about life after death, astrology, or past lives. You could become part of a group or movement dedicated to raising people's awareness.

Monday, January 21 (Moon into Gemini, 9:06 a.m.) It's a number 8 day, your power day, Libra. Focus on a power play. Business discussions go well, especially if you open your mind to a new approach. You're playing with power, so be careful not to hurt others. It's a good day to buy a lotto ticket.

Tuesday, January 22 (Moon in Gemini) You're a dreamer and a thinker now, Libra. You yearn for a new experience. Look to the big picture. Higher education and the higher mind are emphasized. It's a great time to improve your skills in a foreign language.

Wednesday, January 23 (Moon into Cancer, 10:01 p.m.) It's a number 1 day, and you're at the top of your cycle. In romance something new is brewing, if you're interested in pursuing it. Trust your hunches; intuition is highlighted. You get a fresh start. You're inventive and make connections that others overlook. You're determined and courageous today.

Thursday, January 24 (Moon in Cancer) The moon is in your tenth house today. Professional concerns are the focus of the day. You're more emotional and warm than usual toward coworkers. However, be careful not to cross the boundary between your personal and professional lives. You're in the public eye, so avoid overwrought emotional displays.

Friday, January 25 (Moon in Cancer) You're probably feeling somewhat moody today and sensitive to other people's feelings. You're intuitive and nurturing, but you might need to back off for a while and keep things to yourself. It's a good day to work at home.

Saturday, January 26 (Moon into Leo, 9:21 a.m.) With a full moon in your eleventh house, Libra, you hear news about friends or a group. You gain illumination about your dreams and goals, and reap what you've sown.

Sunday, January 27 (Moon in Leo) Yesterday's energy flows into your Sunday as relationships with friends expand into new areas. You find strength in numbers and meaning through friends and groups. Social consciousness plays a role.

Monday, January 28 (Moon into Virgo, 6:28 p.m.)
Service to others is the theme of the day. Diplomacy wins the way. You offer advice and support. Be understanding, and avoid confrontations. A domestic adjustment works out for the best.

Tuesday, January 29 (Moon in Virgo)   The moon is in your twelfth house today. It's a good day to work behind the scenes. Hide your moodiness from others. Take time to reflect and meditate. Unconscious attitudes can be difficult. Things from the past, even your childhood, play a role.

Wednesday, January 30 (Moon in Virgo)   Jupiter goes direct in your ninth house today, suggesting that you see the big picture related to your higher-education goals or your plans for long-distance travel. You can expand a publishing project. Foreign countries play a role.

Thursday, January 31 (Moon into Libra, 1:36 a.m.)
It's a number 9 day. Complete a project now. Clear up odds and ends. Take an inventory on where things are going in your life. Look to the future, and set your goals. It's a good day to make a donation to a worthy cause.

FEBRUARY 2013

Friday, February 1 (Moon in Libra)   Venus moves into your fifth house today, where it stays until February 25. You're feeling playful, sensual, and romantic. You love to be loved, Libra. You're in love with love this month. Meanwhile, Mars moves into your sixth house, suggesting that you're quite aggressive this month in the workplace. Be careful not to offend others with your confrontational and amorous behavior.

Saturday, February 2 (Moon into Scorpio, 7:02 a.m.)
It's a number 8 day, your power day and a good day to buy a lotto ticket. Think big and act big! Unexpected resources come your way. You attract financial success.

Sunday, February 3 (Moon in Scorpio)   The moon is in your second house today. Expect emotional experiences related to money and your values. You have the opportunity now to reevaluate your situation and make important changes. Take the initiative, Libra, and keep your sense of independence. Avoid any large purchases for a few days.

Monday, February 4 (Moon into Sagittarius, 10:46 a.m.)   It's a number 1 day. You're at the top of your cycle. Be independent and creative, and refuse to be discouraged by naysayers. Trust your hunches. You're inventive and make connections that others overlook.

Tuesday, February 5 (Moon in Sagittarius)   Mercury moves into your sixth house today. Others rely on you for help now. You're the one they call upon in time of need. Provide help, but don't deny your own needs. You communicate well, and others understand what they need to do. You're also quick to discuss any health-related issues.

Wednesday, February 6 (Moon into Capricorn, 12:56 p.m.)   Yesterday's energy flows into your Wednesday. You're innovative and creative and communicate well. Enjoy the harmony, beauty, and pleasures of life. Your popularity is on the rise. Your imagination is keen now. Ease up on routines, and spread your good news.

Thursday, February 7 (Moon in Capricorn)   The moon is in your fourth house today. It's an excellent day to step back and reassess everything that's been going on. Take time to meditate and clear your mind. Find a quiet place, preferably at home. You gain energy and support from your family and the home scene now.

Friday, February 8 (Moon into Aquarius, 2:18 p.m.)   It's a number 5 day. Change and variety are highlighted. Approach the day with an unconventional mindset, a new perspective. Take a risk; think outside the box. Promote new ideas; follow your curiosity. A change of scenery would work to your advantage.

Saturday, February 9 (Moon in Aquarius)   The moon is in your fifth house today. Inspiration comes your way. You're feeling creative and expressive. There's greater emotional depth in relationships now. Any dealings with children go well. Pets play a role!

Sunday, February 10 (Moon into Pisces, 4:21 p.m.) There's a new moon in your fifth house today. That means new opportunities arise related to your creative life. You're more emotionally in touch with the creative facets of your life. Alternately, a doorway opens, and a new love interest could enter your life.

Monday, February 11 (Moon in Pisces)   It's a service day. Others rely on you for help now. Do a good deed; make someone happy. But don't deny your own needs. Emotional repression is likely. Keep your resolutions about exercise, and watch your diet.

Tuesday, February 12 (Moon into Aries, 8:53 p.m.) It's a number 9 day. It's a good day to finish up a project, close a door, and get ready to open a new one. Clear up odds and ends, but don't start anything today. Take time to reflect. Look beyond the immediate. Visualize the future; set your goals, then make them so.

Wednesday, February 13 (Moon in Aries)   The moon is in your seventh house today. Partnerships are highlighted. Focus on personal relationships. Loved ones play a major role. Be aware that any conflicts, especially with women, will be more emotional than usual. You could have a difficult time remaining detached and objective.

Thursday, February 14 (Moon in Aries)   It's a great time for initiating projects, launching new ideas, or brainstorming. Emotions could be volatile. You're passionate but impatient. It's a good day for participating or attending an athletic event.

Friday, February 15 (Moon into Taurus, 5:09 a.m.) Take time to relax, enjoy yourself, recharge your batteries. You can influence people now with your upbeat attitude. Your charm and wit are appreciated. Foster generosity. In romance, you're an ardent and loyal lover.

Saturday, February 16 (Moon in Taurus)   The moon is in your eighth house today. Your experiences are more intense than usual. You have a strong sense of duty and feel obligated to fulfill your promises. Security is an important issue with you right now. It's a good day for dealing with mortgages, insurance, and investments.

Sunday, February 17 (Moon into Gemini, 4:51 p.m.) Change and variety are highlighted. Think outside the box. Think freedom, no restrictions. Release old structures; get a new point of view. Promote new ideas; follow your curiosity. But be careful that you don't spread out and diversify too much.

Monday, February 18 (Moon in Gemini)   Saturn goes retrograde in your sixth house today and stays that way until July 7. During this period you're frustrated by delays related to your work. You're willing to take on new responsibilities, but no one seems to be listening. You worry about your situation and are concerncd that a pay increase or contract is taking so long. Be careful that your concerns don't affect your health.

Tuesday, February 19 (Moon in Gemini)   The moon is in your ninth house today. You yearn for new experiences now. You have an interest in new ideas, and you can create positive change through them. You seek something new, a break from the status quo.

Wednesday, February 20 (Moon into Cancer, 5:45 a.m.) It's your power day and your day to play it your way. A risk pays off; expect a windfall. Try a new approach, and expect a financial gain. But remember that you're playing with power, so be careful not to hurt others.

Thursday, February 21 (Moon in Cancer) The moon is in your tenth house today. Business is highlighted. You gain an elevation in prestige. You're more emotional and warm toward coworkers. You're also in the public eye, so avoid any emotional displays.

Friday, February 22 (Moon into Leo, 5:12 p.m.) You're at the top of your cycle again, Libra. Take the lead in a new project, and don't be afraid to turn in a new direction. Experiment and explore. You get a fresh start, a new beginning. Trust your hunches; intuition is highlighted.

Saturday, February 23 (Moon in Leo) Mercury goes retrograde in your sixth house today, where it stays until March 17. There could be some communication breakdown over the next three weeks regarding matters in the workplace. There may also be delays or glitches related to business travel plans. Expect some confusion or misinterpretation when you offer to help others. Best not to sign contracts now. If you must do so, read the small print.

Sunday, February 24 (Moon in Leo)   The moon is in your eleventh house today. You work well with others, especially in a group. Friends play a surprisingly important role, especially Gemini and Aquarius. Focus on your wishes and dreams. Examine your overall goals, and make sure that they're still an expression of who you are.

Monday, February 25 (Moon into Virgo, 1:53 a.m.) There's a full moon in your twelfth house today. You may feel like withdrawing from the action and working behind the scenes. Something from your unconscious mind surfaces, and things become much clearer now. You harvest whatever you've sown. Meanwhile, Venus is moving into your sixth house. That means a flirtation with a fellow worker could turn serious over the next three weeks. Alternately, you may be feeling a strong emotional attachment to the workplace, your job, or fellow workers.

Tuesday, February 26 (Moon in Virgo)   Yesterday's energy flows into your Tuesday. It's a good day to stay out of the public and keep your thoughts to yourself. Be aware of hidden enemies, but think carefully before you act. There's a tendency now to undo all the positive actions you've taken.

Wednesday, February 27 (Moon into Libra, 8:02 a.m.)   Diplomacy wins the way today. Do a good deed for someone. Visit someone who is ill or in need of help. Be sympathetic, kind, and compassionate. But avoid scattering your energies.

Thursday, February 28 (Moon in Libra) With the moon on your ascendant today, you're recharged for the month ahead, and you're more appealing to the public. You're physically vital, and relations with the opposite sex go well. The way you see yourself is the way others see you.

MARCH 2013

Friday, March 1 (Moon into Scorpio, 12:34 p.m.) The month begins on your power day, Libra. You have a good chance now to get a financial boost. Unexpected money arrives. Think big and act big! It's your day to play it your way.

Saturday, March 2 (Moon in Scorpio) With the moon in your second house, you're feeling a sense of abundance. You expand your horizons with a new purchase. A partner may play a role in financial gains. You're in a fortunate position, but don't overextend yourself.

Sunday, March 3 (Moon into Sagittarius, 4:11 p.m.) It's a number 1 day. That means you're at the top of your cycle, Libra. You get a fresh start now. Be independent, and avoid negative people. Surround yourself with creative and adventurous ones. Trust your hunches, and don't be afraid to turn in a new direction.

Monday, March 4 (Moon in Sagittarius) The moon is in your third house today. It's a good day for expressing yourself through writing. Take what you know, and share it with others. As you go about your everyday life, look to the big picture. Expect an invitation to a social event.

Tuesday, March 5 (Moon into Capricorn, 7:15 p.m.)
It's a number 3 day. Your attitude determines everything today. Spread your good news. You're innovative and creative and communicate well. Enjoy the harmony, beauty, and pleasures of life. Beautify your home now, Libra.

Wednesday, March 6 (Moon in Capricorn)   With the moon in your fourth house today, you feel a close tie to your roots. A parent plays a role. Work on a home-improvement project. You're dealing with the foundations of who you are and who you are becoming.

Thursday, March 7 (Moon into Aquarius, 10:03 p.m.)   It's a number 5 day. Promote new ideas; follow your curiosity. Freedom of thought and action is key. A change of scenery would do you good. You're versatile and changeable. However, be careful not to spread out and diversify too much.

Friday, March 8 (Moon in Aquarius)   The moon is in your fifth house today. Your emotions tend to overpower your intellect. It's a good day to take a chance and experiment, especially with a creative project. You feel strongly attached to loved ones, particularly children. But eventually you need to let go.

Saturday, March 9 (Moon in Aquarius)   The moon is in your sixth house of health and daily work.

Keep your resolutions about exercise, and watch your diet. Attend to details related to your health. Make a doctor or dentist appointment, if needed. Your personal health occupies your attention.

Sunday, March 10—Daylight Saving Time Begins (Moon into Pisces, 1:20 a.m.)   It's a number 8 day, your power day. Business dealings go well. You could pull off a financial coup. You're being watched by people in power. Be courageous and honest. Also, be aware that fear of failure can attract tangible experiences that reinforce the feeling.

Monday, March 11 (Moon in Pisces)   There's a new moon in your sixth house today. A doorway opens related to the workplace. You get an opportunity to move ahead, especially if you're providing a service. It's also a good time to pursue a new approach to your health and diet.

Tuesday, March 12 (Moon into Aries, 6:18 a.m.) With Mars moving into Aries, your seventh house, you're all fired up and in an aggressive mode. You need to be careful to avoid spats with a spouse or partner over the next few weeks. Your anger could flare up at a moment's notice. Do your best to remain aware of your emotions rather than let them rule you. Make use of this energy to start something new.

Wednesday, March 13 (Moon in Aries)   The moon is in your seventh house today. The focus turns to relationships, business and personal ones. You get along well with others now. You can fit in just about anywhere. Loved ones and partners are more important than usual in helping you move ahead on whatever you're doing.

Thursday, March 14 (Moon into Taurus, 2:09 p.m.)
Your organizational skills are called upon now. You're building foundations for the future, developing outlets for your creativity. Emphasize quality in whatever you're doing. Be methodical and thorough, and don't wander off task.

Friday, March 15 (Moon in Taurus)   The moon is in your eighth house today. Things could get emotionally intense in your dealings with someone from the opposite sex. That's particularly true if you're facing issues related to shared belongings. You're sensitive and intuitive, and you could take an interest in a metaphysical topic, such as past lives.

Saturday, March 16 (Moon in Taurus)   Security is an important issue with you right now. It can affect your feelings about your possessions, as well as things that you share with others, such as a spouse. It's a good day for dealing with mortgages, insurance, and investments. Meanwhile, mysteries of the unknown attract your attention, distracting you from more mundane activities.

Sunday, March 17 (Moon into Gemini, 1:10 a.m.)
Mercury goes direct in your ninth house today. Confusion, miscommunication, and delays related to long-distance travel or higher education recede into the past. Things move more smoothly. You get your message

across. Delays related to making arrangement for travel or classes come to an end. Everything works better, including computers and other electronic equipment.

Monday, March 18 (Moon in Gemini)   The moon and Mercury are both in your ninth house today as yesterday's energy flows into your Monday. A foreign country or person of foreign birth could play a romantic role. Publicity and advertising are emphasized. It's also a good time to pursue an interest in philosophy, mythology, or comparative religions.

Tuesday, March 19 (Moon into Cancer, 1:56 p.m.) It's a number 9 day, a good day to finish up a project and get ready for something new. Visualize the future; set your goals, then make them so. But don't start anything until tomorrow.

Wednesday, March 20 (Moon in Cancer)   You're feeling restless and busy trying to get your message across. You're e-mailing, texting friends, posting on Facebook, and making calls. It's a good day to get together with friends for lunch or meet them at a bookstore or coffee shop. A change of scenery works wonders now.

Thursday, March 21 (Moon in Cancer)   Venus moves into Aries, your seventh house, today, where it stays for three weeks. It's time for a new beginning, especially in romance and partnerships. It's a good time for a wedding. You live for relationships now and want to spend more time with a partner. Others find you attractive and charming.

Friday, March 22 (Moon into Leo, 1:50 a.m.)   It's a number 2 day. That means that cooperation and partnership are highlighted again. There's a new beginning or a new opportunity arises. Your intuition focuses on relationships. Don't make waves. Don't rush or show resentment; let things develop.

Saturday, March 23 (Moon in Leo)   Friends play an important role in your day, especially Gemini and Aquarius. You work well with group of like-minded individuals. At the same time, you emphasize your individuality. Focus on your wishes and dreams. Examine your overall goals. Those goals should be an expression of who you are.

Sunday, March 24 (Moon into Virgo, 10:50 a.m.) It's a number 4 day. Your organizational skills are highlighted today. Control your impulses. Take care of your obligations. You're building foundations for an outlet for your creativity. Emphasize quality. Be methodical and thorough.

Monday, March 25 (Moon in Virgo)   The moon is in your twelfth house today. You might feel a need to withdraw and work behind the scenes, where you'll feel more grounded. Things concerning the past, even your childhood, play a role. It's best to hide your emotions and moodiness. Be aware that a secret enemy might have entered the mix.

Tuesday, March 26 (Moon into Libra, 4:33 p.m.) It's a service day, Libra. Take time to help someone close to you. You have a strong sense of duty and feel obligated to fulfill your promises. A change in the home, an adjustment or readjustment, is needed now. Don't put off the situation; that will only aggravate the problem. Be diplomatic, and focus on making people happy.

Wednesday, March 27 (Moon in Libra)   There's a full moon in your first house today. You gain insight into your personal life, possibly by taking time to meditate. It's a time of completion. Your face is in front of the public. You reap what you've sown. Your feelings and thoughts are aligned, and you're recharged for the month ahead.

Thursday, March 28 (Moon into Scorpio, 7:55 p.m.) It's a number 8 day, your power day, and your day to play it your way. Open your mind to a new approach that could bring in big bucks. Business dealings go well. However, you're playing with power, so be careful not to hurt others.

Friday, March 29 (Moon in Scorpio)   The moon is in your second house today. You tend to equate your financial assets with emotional security now. You feel best surrounded by your stuff. It's not the objects themselves that are important, but the feelings and memories you associate with them. Put off making any major purchases.

Saturday, March 30 (Moon into Sagittarius, 10:14 p.m.)   It's a number 1 day, and you're at the top of your cycle again. You get a fresh start, a new beginning. You're inventive and make connections that others overlook. Don't be afraid to turn in a new direction. Be independent and creative.

Sunday, March 31 (Moon in Sagittarius) The moon is in your third house today, Libra. Your mental abilities are strong now, and you have an emotional need to reinvigorate your studies, especially regarding matters of the past. Take what you know, and share it with others. You help keep everyone around you in balance. It's also a good day for a challenging mental activity, such as on-line gaming, a debate, or a game of chess, anything that challenges your mental prowess.

APRIL 2013

Monday, April 1 (Moon in Sagittarius) The moon is in your third house today, Libra. You're busy keeping your mind occupied with new information. You study the details, especially those that relate to the past. You write from a deep place. It's a good day for journaling. You could be dealing with siblings, other relatives, or neighbors. You accept an invitation to a social event.

Tuesday, April 2 (Moon into Capricorn, 12:36 a.m.) Get out and meet new people, have new experiences, do something you've never done before. Stress originality in whatever you do. You're determined and courageous today. You attract creative people. In romance a flirtation turns more serious.

Wednesday, April 3 (Moon in Capricorn) Some of yesterday's energy flows into your Wednesday.

Spend time with your family and other loved ones. Stick close to home. You're dealing with the foundations of who you are and who you are becoming. Retreat to a private place for meditation. It's a good day for dream recall. A parent plays a role.

Thursday, April 4 (Moon into Aquarius, 3:42 a.m.)
You're creative and express yourself well today. Your intuition and artistic talents are highlighted, Libra. You communicate well. You're warm and receptive to what others say. Spread your good news, and take time to listen to others. Your attitude determines everything.

Friday, April 5 (Moon in Aquarius)   The moon is in your fifth house today. Your love life takes off now. There's an idealistic turn to whatever you do for pleasure. It's a great time for a creative project, especially fiction writing. You could be somewhat possessive of loved ones and children. A pet could also play a role.

Saturday, April 6 (Moon into Pisces, 8:01 a.m.)
It's a number 5 day. You're restless and looking for change, a new perspective. You're versatile and changeable, but be careful not to overcommit yourself now. Stay focused as best you can. Take risks; experiment. Pursue a new idea. Freedom of thought and action is key.

Sunday, April 7 (Moon in Pisces)   With the moon in your sixth house on this Sunday, the emphasis turns to service to others. Attend to all the details, and keep everyone around you in balance, Libra. Be careful not to overlook any seemingly minor matters that could take on importance. Keep up with your exercise plan, and watch your diet.

Monday, April 8 (Moon into Aries, 2:03 p.m.) It's a number 7 day. You investigate, analyze, or simply observe what's going on now. You quickly come to a conclusion and wonder why others don't see what you see. You detect deception and recognize insincerity with ease.

Tuesday, April 9 (Moon in Aries) The moon is in your seventh house today. You could be negotiating or signing a contract now, possibly for the sale of your house. You're taking the initiative with your partner, and emotions could get volatile. It's difficult to maintain an objective and detached point of view. Be careful not to let others manipulate your feelings.

Wednesday, April 10 (Moon into Taurus, 10:22 p.m.) There's a new moon in Aries, your seventh house, today, along with six planets. It's all about opportunities that come your way related to partnerships and contracts. It's a great time for setting off on a joint venture. You have the cosmos working in your favor, especially if you're starting something new. Whatever comes your way now, the energy is strong and could dramatically change your life.

Thursday, April 11 (Moon in Taurus) The moon is in your eighth house today. You attract the attention of powerful people. Be aware that your experiences could be more intense than usual. You could be dealing with a matter related to shared belongings, investments, or taxes. An interest in metaphysics plays a role. You could be reading about concepts of life after death.

Friday, April 12 (Moon in Taurus)   Pluto goes retrograde in your fourth house today and stays that way until September 9. That means things get bogged down related to your home life or property. If you're selling your home, there could be delays. The same is true related to any plans for renovations. No matter how hard you try to help a family member or someone in your home, it takes longer than expected to accomplish whatever you're trying to achieve. You tend to look inward more often and consider whether or not you're doing the right thing regarding a domestic matter.

Saturday, April 13 (Moon into Gemini, 9:13 a.m.) Mercury moves into your seventh house today. You relate well to the public and get your ideas across. You're also good at working with people and arbitrating any disputes, Libra. Sales and public relations are highlighted.

Sunday, April 14 (Moon in Gemini)   With the moon in your ninth house, it's a good day to get away from your usual routine. You're feeling restless. Plan a long trip or sign up for a seminar or workshop that interests you. A publishing project goes well. A foreign-born person might play a role.

Monday, April 15 (Moon into Cancer, 9:50 p.m.) Venus moves into your eighth house today, where it stays until May 9. That indicates that you gain financially now through a marriage or partnership. You could be in a position to control or manipulate another person's money. Alternately, you could join a social movement to improve the well-being of others.

Tuesday, April 16 (Moon in Cancer)   The moon is in your tenth house today. Professional concerns are the focus of the day. You gain an elevation in prestige or a promotion. You get along well with fellow workers, who are appreciative. You're in the public eye, so it's best to avoid any emotional displays.

Wednesday, April 17 (Moon in Cancer)   You're intuitive and nurturing today, Libra. Your home life is important to you. You also could feel moody and overly sensitive. Get out and take a walk. Beautify your house or take care of home repairs. It's a good day to snuggle with your loved one.

Thursday, April 18 (Moon into Leo, 10:15 a.m.)
It's a number 8 day, your power day, your day to play it your way. Expect a financial windfall. It's a good day to play the lotto. Business dealings go well, and a new approach brings in extra income.

Friday, April 19 (Moon in Leo)   With the moon in your eleventh house today, friends play an important role, especially Aquarius and Gemini. Take a look at your goals, and make sure that they're still an expression of who you are. You do well in a group setting, especially if you're dealing with an issue involving social consciousness.

Saturday, April 20 (Moon into Virgo, 8:10 p.m.)
Mars moves into your eighth house today and stays
there until May 31. You tend to get aggressive and
defensive now, especially related to shared income or
possessions. You might have a tendency to dominate
or control a partner's possessions or financial assets.
You take action related to a tax matter, a mortgage,
insurance, or credit cards. Avoid any tendency toward
greediness. It's best to back off and avoid a major
squabble with your partner.

Sunday, April 21 (Moon in Virgo)   The moon is
in your twelfth house today. It's a good day to work
behind the scenes and avoid any conflict. You could
be dealing with a matter from the past that has returned to haunt you. Keep your feelings secret. Follow
your intuition.

Monday, April 22 (Moon in Virgo)   Take care of
details now, especially related to your health. Exercise, and watch your diet. Stop worrying and fretting.
It's a good day to stick close to home. Attend to details, and take care of loose ends.

Tuesday, April 23 (Moon into Libra, 2:26 a.m.)
Get everything in order now, and take care of your
obligations. You're building foundations for an outlet
for your creativity. Emphasize quality in whatever
you're doing. Clear your desk, straighten up your
work area. Tear down the old in order to rebuild.

Wednesday, April 24 (Moon in Libra)   The moon
is in your first house today and on your ascendant.

The way you see yourself now is the way others see you. You're recharged for the month ahead, and this makes you more appealing to the public. You're physically vital, and relations with the opposite sex go well.

Thursday, April 25 (Moon into Scorpio, 5:27 a.m.) There's a lunar eclipse in your second house today. You gain insight into a financial matter. Your concerns about security play a role. If you feel that you need to take charge, make sure you control your emotions. Inform others of your plans. Whatever the issue that comes up, it's a serious one.

Friday, April 26 (Moon in Scorpio) Yesterday's concerns about finances continue into your Friday. Expect emotional experiences related to money. You feel best when surrounded by familiar objects in your home environment. It's not the objects themselves that are important, but the feelings and memories you associate with them. Put off making any major purchases.

Saturday, April 27 (Moon into Sagittarius, 6:33 a.m.) It's a number 8 day, your power day. Business dealings go well. You could pull off a financial coup now. You're being watched by people in power. Be courageous and honest. Also, be aware that fear of failure can attract tangible experiences that reinforce the feeling.

Sunday, April 28 (Moon in Sagittarius) The moon is in your third house today. You have an emotional need to pursue ideas and subjects that interest you. Your intellectual curiosity requires continued nurturing. Meanwhile, you're dealing with siblings, other relatives, or neighbors. Express your opinions, but stay in control of your emotions.

Monday, April 29 (Moon into Capricorn, 7:22 a.m.)
It's a number 1 day. You're at the top of your cycle. You get a fresh start, a new beginning. Get out and meet new people, have new experiences, do something you've never done before. You're inventive and make connections that others overlook. Stress originality.

Tuesday, April 30 (Moon in Capricorn) The moon is in your fourth house, Libra. It's a good day to take the day off or work at home. You're seeking harmony and peace on the domestic scene. Find time for a home-repair project. You could be dealing with parents now. You feel a close tie to your roots.

MAY 2013

Wednesday, May 1 (Moon into Aquarius, 9:20 a.m.)
Mercury moves into your eighth house today, where it stays until May 15. You exchange messages as you communicate with a partner about resources that you share. Meanwhile, your mind is much more open than usual to the occult. You could even have a ghost-sighting experience.

Thursday, May 2 (Moon in Aquarius) The moon is in your fifth house today. Be yourself; be emotionally honest. In love there's greater emotional depth to a relationship now. You're emotionally in touch with your creative side. It's a good day to take a chance, experiment.

Friday, May 3 (Moon into Pisces, 1:26 p.m.)   It's a number 3 day. You're innovative and creative and communicate well today, Libra. It's your kind of day. Enjoy the harmony, beauty, and pleasures of life. Your attitude determines everything. Strut your stuff. Spread your good news.

Saturday, May 4 (Moon in Pisces)   The moon is in your sixth house today. It's a service day, Libra. Others come to you for help. You improve and refine what they started. You keep everything and everyone in balance. Offer help, but don't deny your own needs. Take care of any health issues.

Sunday, May 5 (Moon into Aries, 8:04 p.m.)   Freedom of thought and action is key today. But so is moderation; avoid excess in whatever you're doing. You're seeking new horizons, a new perspective, but you tend to lack order and discipline. It's all about travel, adventure, and meeting new people.

Monday, May 6 (Moon in Aries)   The moon is in your seventh house today. The focus turns to relationships, both business and personal ones. You get along well with others now, and look for ways to expand a relationship. You can fit in just about anywhere. Loved ones and partners are more important than usual. But be careful that others don't manipulate your feelings.

Tuesday, May 7 (Moon in Aries)   It's a great day for initiating projects, launching new ideas, or brainstorming. You're passionate but impatient. You could also be somewhat reckless today, so be careful where you step. You're extremely persuasive, especially if you're passionate about what you're doing, selling, or trying to convey. Athletics or sporting events could play a role in your day.

Wednesday, May 8 (Moon into Taurus, 5:10 a.m.) It's a number 8 day, a good day to buy a lotto ticket. It's your power day, your day to play it your way. You can go far with your plans and achieve financial success. Unexpected money comes your way. Expect financial success now.

Thursday, May 9 (Moon in Taurus)   Venus moves into your ninth house today, where it stays until June 2. You have a love of long-distance travel and studying history or matters from the past. There's also a solar eclipse in your eighth house. That means new opportunities come knocking related to shared income or resources. You could also get a chance to explore the mysterious and unknown.

Friday, May 10 (Moon into Gemini, 4:22 p.m.) It's a number 1 day, and you're at the top of your cycle again. Be bold and creative. Trust your hunches; intuition is highlighted. Stress independence and originality in whatever actions you're taking or decisions you're making. In romance something new is developing.

Saturday, May 11 (Moon in Gemini)   The moon is in your ninth house today. You're a dreamer and a thinker. You may feel a need to get away now, a break from the usual routine. You yearn for a new experience. Higher education or long-distance travel plays a role.

Sunday, May 12 (Moon in Gemini)   You're feeling restless today and sending text messages to friends and associates to pass the time. Your mind moves quickly from one thought to another. You might be completing tasks faster than others do, and they could have trouble keeping up with you. You see both sides of an issue, and you try to keep everyone in balance.

Monday, May 13 (Moon into Cancer, 4:58 a.m.) Your organizational skills are highlighted today. Control your impulses. Take care of your obligations. You're building foundations for an outlet for your creativity. Emphasize quality in whatever you're doing. Be methodical and thorough.

Tuesday, May 14 (Moon in Cancer)   The moon is in your tenth house today. It's a good day for sales and dealing with the public. You get a boost in prestige. You get along with fellow workers, and you're sensitive to their needs.

Wednesday, May 15 (Moon into Leo, 5:39 p.m.) It's a service day, and you could be helping someone close to you. You serve, teach, and guide. But know when to say enough is enough. Clear up a situation at home that has lingered too long. Be diplomatic, and focus on making people happy.

Thursday, May 16 (Moon in Leo)   The moon is in your eleventh house today. Friends play an important role in your day, especially Gemini and Aquarius. You get along well with a group of like-minded people, especially if you're working for the common good. Take time to focus on your wishes and dreams.

Friday, May 17 (Moon in Leo)   You're at center stage today, Libra. Be wild and imaginative; be the person you always imagined you might be. Play with different personae. Theatrics and drama are highlighted. You're creative and passionate, impulsive and honest.

Saturday, May 18 (Moon into Virgo, 4:34 a.m.) Your individuality is stressed today, and your visionary abilities are heightened. You have a greater sense of freedom, a new perspective. You're dealing with new ideas, new options. Play your hunches. Look beyond the immediate.

Sunday, May 19 (Moon in Virgo)   The moon is in your twelfth house today. Unconscious attitudes can be difficult; so can relations with women. Keep your feelings to yourself. Be aware of hidden enemies. It's a great day for a mystical or spiritual discipline. Your intuition is heightened.

Monday, May 20 (Moon into Libra, 12:08 p.m.) Your emotions and sensitivity are highlighted. Marriage or a partnership plays a key role now. The spotlight is on cooperation. Use your intuition to get a sense of the day. There could be some soul searching related to relationships, or a new relationship could be forming.

Tuesday, May 21 (Moon in Libra)   With the moon in your first house, Libra, it's all about your health and your emotional self: how you feel and how you feel about yourself. You feelings tend to fluctuate by the moment. You could spend time either procrastinating or changing your plans. You focus on how the public relates to you.

Wednesday, May 22 (Moon into Scorpio, 3:56 p.m.) The moon is in your second house today. Money and material goods are important to you and give you a sense of security. You identify emotionally with your possessions or whatever you value. Watch your spending. You have a tendency to collect things, and those objects make you feel at home and at peace.

Thursday, May 23 (Moon in Scorpio)   Expect intense, emotional experiences today. You're passionate, and your sexuality is heightened. Investigate, research, dig deep for information. Be aware of things happening in secret and of possible deception.

Friday, May 24 (Moon into Sagittarius, 4:50 p.m.) It's a number 6 day, your day to help others. Be understanding, and avoid confrontations. Diplomacy wins the way. Focus on making people happy, but avoid scattering your energies. Be sympathetic, kind, and compassionate.

Saturday, May 25 (Moon in Sagittarius)   There's a lunar eclipse in your third house today. It's a good day for expressing yourself through writing. You gain insight about a matter that's important to you. It could involve something from the past and cause a strong emotional reaction. Take what you know, and share it with others, especially siblings and other relatives. As you go about your everyday life, look to the big picture.

Sunday, May 26 (Moon into Capricorn, 4:29 p.m.) It's a number 8 day, another power day. Open your mind to a new approach. Unexpected resources arrive. You can go far with your plans and achieve financial success. But be aware that you're playing with power, so try not to hurt anyone.

Monday, May 27 (Moon in Capricorn)   The moon is in your fourth house today. You feel close to your roots now. Spend time with your family and loved ones. Stick close to home, if possible. A parent plays a role. It's a good day to work on a home-repair project.

Tuesday, May 28 (Moon into Aquarius, 4:49 p.m.) It's a number 1 day, and you're at the top of your cycle again. Get out and meet new people, have new experiences, do something you've never done before. In romance something new is developing. Explore, discover, create. Trust your hunches.

Wednesday, May 29 (Moon in Aquarius)   The moon is in your fifth house today. It's a good day for pursuing a romance. There's greater emotional depth in whatever you choose. You're creative now and have the ability to tap deeply into the collective unconscious. Children and pets could play a role.

Thursday, May 30 (Moon into Pisces, 7:31 p.m.) Your attitude determines everything today, Libra. You communicate well. You're curious and inventive; ideas bubble forth. Your imagination is keen now. Your popularity is on the rise.

Friday, May 31 (Moon in Pisces) Mercury moves into your tenth house today, where it stays until June 27. Business dealings are highlighted. You communicate well. It's a great time for sales and promotions and getting yourself into public view. You get an elevation in prestige. Meanwhile, Mars moves into your ninth house today, where it remains until July 13. That means you can become more aggressive now in your pursuit of higher education or long-distance travel.

JUNE 2013

Saturday, June 1 (Moon in Pisces) The moon is in your sixth house today. Others rely on you for help, Libra, but it's about time for you to dance to your own tune. Avoid falling into a martyr syndrome. Don't let your fears hold you back. Take care of any health or diet issues.

Sunday, June 2 (Moon into Aries, 1:34 a.m.) Venus moves into your tenth house today and stays there until June 27. That means your career and professional goals move ahead smoothly now. You could get a raise or an advancement. You love what you're doing and get along well with fellow workers. You also could get involved romantically with someone who shares the same career.

Monday, June 3 (Moon in Aries)   The moon is in your ruling seventh house today, Libra. Loved ones and partners are more important than usual. You get along well with others now. You can fit in just about anywhere. Women play a prominent role. A legal matter comes to your attention.

Tuesday, June 4 (Moon into Taurus, 10:55 a.m.) It's a number 5 day. That means it's a good day to promote new ideas. You're versatile, changeable. Be careful not to spread out and diversify too much. Freedom of thought and action is key. A change of scenery would work to your advantage.

Wednesday, June 5 (Moon in Taurus)   With the moon in your eighth house today, Libra, your experiences are more intense than usual. Security takes on new importance, and you're especially concerned about shared possessions. A mortgage, inheritance, or insurance policy could play a role. You also could be pursuing a metaphysical matter that interests you.

Thursday, June 6 (Moon into Gemini, 10:33 p.m.) Neptune goes retrograde in your sixth house today and stays that way until November 13. There could be some difficulties related to the workplace or your efforts to help others. Something secretive and deceptive is going on. Move with care when discussing your plans. You also could get bogged down worrying about your health or diet.

Friday, June 7 (Moon in Gemini) The moon is in your ninth house today. Higher education and long-distance travel are key elements of your day—one or both. You're a dreamer and a thinker now. You may feel a need to get away, a break from the usual routine. You yearn for a new experience.

Saturday, June 8 (Moon in Gemini) There's a new moon in your ninth house today. You can create positive change through your ideas. New opportunities come your way related to long-distance travel or higher education. You have a good chance to expand on whatever you're doing, especially if it relates to education or foreign lands. A foreign-born person could offer you a unique opportunity.

Sunday, June 9 (Moon into Cancer, 11:17 a.m.) You're at the top of your cycle, Libra. You get a fresh start. Your intuition is highlighted. You're inventive and make connections that others overlook. Get out and meet new people. You attract creative individuals now. Explore and discover.

Monday, June 10 (Moon in Cancer) The moon is in your tenth house today. Professional concerns occupy your thoughts. It's a good day for dealing with the public. You get along well with coworkers now, but be careful about mixing your personal life with your professional world.

Tuesday, June 11 (Moon into Leo, 11:59 p.m.)   It's a number 3 day. Make use of your charm and wit. Your popularity is on the rise. Ease up on your routines. Attend a cultural event, such as an art gallery or museum opening. Make time to listen to others, and spread your good news. Your intuition is highlighted.

Wednesday, June 12 (Moon in Leo)   With the moon in your eleventh house today, Libra, you find strength in numbers and opportunities through friends and groups. You have a good chance now to achieve your wishes and dreams. Your sense of security is tied to your relationships and friends.

Thursday, June 13 (Moon in Leo)   Everything seems grand and majestic now. You're creative and passionate today, impulsive and honest. Showmanship is emphasized in whatever you're doing. Drama plays a role, perhaps involving children. Animals and pets figure prominently.

Friday, June 14 (Moon into Virgo, 11:26 a.m.)   It's a service day. Focus on making people happy and keeping everyone in balance, Libra. You seek harmony and peace. Be sympathetic, kind, and compassionate. However, avoid scattering your energies.

Saturday, June 15 (Moon in Virgo)   The moon is in your twelfth house today. It's a good time to step back and withdraw from the action. Keep your feelings secret as you work behind the scenes. Relations with women can be difficult now. It's a great day for a mystical or spiritual discipline. Your intuition is heightened.

Sunday, June 16 (Moon into Libra, 8:19 p.m.) It's your power day and your day to play it your way. You have a chance to expand, to gain recognition, fame, and power. Keep in mind that you're playing with power; be careful not to hurt others.

Monday, June 17 (Moon in Libra) The moon is on your ascendant. The focus is on your appearance and how you are perceived by the public. The way you see yourself now is the way others see you. You're recharged for the month ahead, and this makes you more appealing to the public. You're physically vital, and relations with the opposite sex go well.

Tuesday, June 18 (Moon in Libra) You're feeling sensitive and dealing with your sense of who you are and who you are becoming. It's all about your emotional self. Your thoughts and feelings are aligned. You're at center stage now. Self-awareness and appearance are important.

Wednesday, June 19 (Moon into Scorpio, 1:39 a.m.) It's a number 2 day. The spotlight is on cooperative efforts and partnerships. Be kind and understanding, patient and supportive. Let things develop. Don't make waves; don't rush or show resentment.

Thursday, June 20 (Moon in Scorpio) The moon is in your second house. It's a great day for investments. You feel emotionally secure when surrounded by your belongings. It's not the objects themselves that are important, but the feelings and memories you associate with them. Avoid making any major purchases today.

Friday, June 21 (Moon into Sagittarius, 3:31 a.m.)
It's a number 4 day. Your organizational skills come into play today. Stay focused; emphasize quality. Be methodical and thorough. There could be a tendency to be stubborn.

Saturday, June 22 (Moon in Sagittarius) The moon is in your third house today. You write from a deep place. It's a good day for journaling. Your thinking may be unduly influenced by things from the past. Visits by relatives or siblings are likely; so is contact with neighbors. You accept an invitation to a social event.

Sunday, June 23 (Moon into Capricorn, 3:09 a.m.)
There's a full moon in your fourth house today. It's a good time to complete a project related to your home. Spend time with your family and other loved ones. Stick close to home. With Pluto conjunct, you can now integrate the knowledge that you are the person you've always wanted to be.

Monday, June 24 (Moon in Capricorn) Your ambition and drive to succeed are highlighted. Your responsibilities increase. But you may be feeling stressed and overworked. Self-discipline and structure are key. Don't overlook your exercise routine.

Tuesday, June 25 (Moon into Aquarius, 2:28 a.m.)
Jupiter moves into your tenth house today, where it

stays until mid-July 2014. Over the next year you should see opportunities for expansion related to your career or profession. You get along well with co-workers, especially Aquarius and Gemini. Doors will open. You gain a boost in your prestige.

Wednesday, June 26 (Moon in Aquarius)   Mercury goes retrograde in your tenth house today and stays there until July 20. In spite of yesterday's powerful connection with Jupiter, the new energy is slow in manifesting. Expect delays and glitches in communication over the next three weeks, especially in dealings with coworkers. You're expecting good things to come your way related to your career, and they will. But give it time. Maintain your balance, Libra.

Thursday, June 27 (Moon into Pisces, 3:33 a.m.) Venus moves into your eleventh house today. You put others at ease now in social situations, Libra. You benefit from friends and social contacts and work smoothly with a group, especially if you're dealing with something artistic and creative.

Friday, June 28 (Moon in Pisces)   The moon is in your sixth house today. It's another service day, Libra. If someone in your home environment could use a helping hand or needs your advice, be there for that person. Help others, but dance to your own tune. You improve, edit, and refine the work of others.

Saturday, June 29 (Moon into Aries, 8:08 a.m.) It's a number 3 day. Your attitude determines everything today. Spread your good news. You're innovative and creative and communicate well. Enjoy the harmony, beauty, and pleasures of life. Beautify your home now, Libra.

Sunday, June 30 (Moon in Aries)   With the moon in your ruling seventh house today, you get along well with others. You can fit in just about anywhere. Loved ones and partners are more important than usual. Women play a particularly prominent role.

JULY 2013

Monday, July 1 (Moon into Taurus, 4:44 p.m.) Your imagination is keen now. You're curious and inventive. You communicate well today. Remain flexible. Your attitude determines everything.

Tuesday, July 2 (Moon in Taurus)   The moon is in your eighth house today. Your experiences are more intense and can affect your attitudes toward things you possess or share with others. You have a strong sense of duty and feel obligated to fulfill your promises. Security is an important issue with you right now. You could find yourself managing or controlling the assets of another person. Alternately, you could be dealing with a mystery of the unknown, such as life after death.

Wednesday, July 3 (Moon in Taurus)   You're feeling strong willed today, so be aware that you might be somewhat stubborn and resistant to change. It's a good day to use common sense and take a down-to-earth perspective on whatever you're doing.

Thursday, July 4 (Moon into Gemini, 4:23 a.m.)
It's a number 6 day. Service to others is the theme of
the day. You offer advice and support. Be kind and
helpful; try to avoid confrontations. Be diplomatic
with anyone who is giving you a hard time. Meanwhile, think independence.

Friday, July 5 (Moon in Gemini)   The moon is in
your ninth house today. You're feeling restless, and it's
a good day to make your escape. Or at least plan for
it. Research a destination for a long journey. Alternately, sign up for a workshop or seminar. A publishing project moves ahead.

Saturday, July 6 (Moon into Cancer, 5:14 p.m.)
It's a number 8 day. That means it's your power day.
Be courageous; take a chance. Business dealings go
well. Expect a financial coup. You have a chance today
to expand, to gain recognition, even fame.

Sunday, July 7 (Moon in Cancer)   Saturn turns
direct in your second house today and stays there for
a year and a half. That means that over the coming
months issues could develop related to your finances.
You also could face difficulties related to collecting
what's owed to you or paying out what you owe. Keep
close tabs on how you spend your money, and look for
ways to enhance the base or foundation of your income.

Monday, July 8 (Moon in Cancer)   There's a new
moon in your tenth house. New opportunities come
your way related to your career. You're more open

and accessible now, but take care to avoid emotional displays, especially in public. With four planets also in your tenth house, you get a fresh start, a new beginning. Expect a raise or an advancement.

Tuesday, July 9 (Moon into Leo, 5:48 a.m.)   Use your intuition to get a sense of your day. Cooperation and partnerships are highlighted. Concentrate more on your relationships with others. It's good to build those friendships and to offer support where it is needed. Don't make waves. Don't rush or show resentment; let things develop.

Wednesday, July 10 (Moon in Leo)   You work well with a group of like-minded individuals. At the same time, you emphasize your individuality. You find strength in numbers and meaning through friends and groups. Focus on your wishes and dreams. Examine your overall goals. Make sure that these goals are still an expression of who you are.

Thursday, July 11 (Moon into Virgo, 5:12 p.m.) It's a number 4 day. Your organizational skills are highlighted today. Control your impulses. Take care of your obligations. You're building foundations for an outlet for your creativity. Emphasize quality. Be methodical and thorough.

Friday, July 12 (Moon in Virgo)   The moon is in your twelfth house today. You might feel a need to withdraw and work behind the scenes, where you'll feel more grounded. Things concerning the past, even your childhood, play a role. It's best to hide your emotions and moodiness. Be aware that a secret enemy might've entered the mix.

Saturday, July 13 (Moon in Virgo)   Mars moves into your tenth house today. Even though it's Saturday, there's no stopping you. You're energetic, active, and forceful related to a career move. You could be starting something new and feeling enthusiastic. However, be careful to avoid acting rashly, being inconsiderate, or overly assertive.

Sunday, July 14 (Moon into Libra, 2:41 a.m.) You're looking for the truth about a matter today. It could be related to a personal issue, possibly related to your health or emotional self. You investigate and dig deep. Secrets, intrigue, confidential information play a role. Be aware of decisions made behind closed doors.

Monday, July 15 (Moon in Libra)   You're sensitive to other people's feelings. You may feel moody one moment, happy the next, then withdrawn and sad. Your feelings tend to fluctuate by the moment. Your feelings and thoughts are aligned. You focus on how the public relates to you. You could spend time either procrastinating or changing your plans. It's difficult to remain detached and objective now.

Tuesday, July 16 (Moon into Scorpio, 9:25 a.m.) It's a number 9 day. Clear your desk for tomorrow's new cycle. Accept what comes your way now, but hold off on beginning anything until tomorrow. Take an inventory on where things are going in your life as you clear up odds and ends.

Wednesday, July 17 (Moon in Scorpio)   Uranus goes retrograde in your seventh house today, where it stays until December 17. That means you might be doing some soul searching related to partnerships, personal or business ones. You could be getting flashes of inspiration related to what you really want to do and who you want to do it with. Matters are somewhat unpredictable over the next few months, especially related to relationships and contracts. Avoid going to extremes. Pushing yourself too hard could result in accidents. Watch your step!

Thursday, July 18 (Moon into Sagittarius, 12:55 p.m.) It's a number 2 day, and that means cooperation is highlighted. Use your intuition to focus on relationships, especially partnerships. Don't rush or show resentment; let things develop. Be kind and understanding.

Friday, July 19 (Moon in Sagittarius)   With the moon in your third house today, your mental abilities are strong, Libra, and you have an emotional need to reinvigorate your studies, especially regarding matters of the past. You're attracted to historical or archaeological studies. Take what you know, and share it, but don't expect others to be as excited as you are about delving into the past.

Saturday, July 20 (Moon into Capricorn, 1:40 p.m.) With Mercury going direct in your tenth house today, your mind is sharp, Libra, and you're mentally competitive, especially when you come up with new ideas that help others. Blockages and delays are over, and you've got no time for delays. You want everything to happen now. It's one of those days.

Sunday, July 21 (Moon in Capricorn)   Spend time with your family and other loved ones. Stick close to home. You're dealing with the foundations of who you are and who you are becoming. Don't be surprised if you receive lots of phone calls from family members who live far away. They could be finalizing plans for a family reunion. Take time to beautify your home.

Monday, July 22 (Moon into Aquarius, 1:08 p.m.) With the full moon in Aquarius today, you reap what you've sown related to finances. It's a good day for dealing with money issues. Meanwhile, Venus moves into your ninth house, where it stays until August 17. You may feel a need to get away now, a break from the usual routine. You yearn for a new experience. Focus on new ideas, higher education, or a foreign destination.

Tuesday, July 23 (Moon in Aquarius)   The moon is in your fifth house today. Your emotions tend to overpower your intellect. Be yourself; be emotionally honest. In love, there's greater emotional depth to a relationship now. Creativity is emphasized.

Wednesday, July 24 (Moon into Pisces, 1:23 p.m.) It's a number 8 day, your power day. So focus on a power play. You can go far with your plans and achieve financial success. Open your mind to a new approach that could bring in big bucks. It's a good day to buy a lotto ticket.

Thursday, July 25 (Moon in Pisces)   The moon is in your sixth house today. Your personal health occupies your attention. Keep your resolutions about exercise, and watch your diet. Attend to details related to your making a doctor or dentist appointment. Help others, but don't deny your own needs.

Friday, July 26 (Moon into Aries, 4:30 p.m.)   It's a number 1 day, so you're at the top of your cycle. It's a great time for initiating new projects, launching new ideas, or brainstorming for new ways of making money. You take the lead on something as you get a fresh start. Follow your heart.

Saturday, July 27 (Moon in Aries)   The moon is in your seventh house today. You get along well with others. You can fit in just about anywhere. Loved ones and partners are more important than usual. You comprehend the nuances of a situation, but it's difficult to go with the flow. Be careful that others don't manipulate your feelings.

Sunday, July 28 (Moon into Taurus, 11:44 p.m.)   Have fun today in preparation for tomorrow's discipline and focus. Make time to listen to others. Your charm and wit are appreciated. Spread your good news; you communicate well.

Monday, July 29 (Moon in Taurus)   The moon is in your eighth house today. Your experiences are more intense than usual, especially when dealing with matters related to your home. It's a good day to deal with a mortgage, insurance, credit cards, or investment. Take time to meditate or study a metaphysical subject, such as life after death or reincarnation.

Tuesday, July 30 (Moon in Taurus)   Cultivate new ideas, but make sure that they're down to earth. Use your common sense, and do practical things. Health and physical activity are highlighted. Try to avoid stubborn behavior when others question your actions. You could be somewhat possessive now.

Wednesday, July 31 (Moon into Gemini, 10:42 a.m.) It's a number 6 day. Focus on making people happy. Service to others is the theme of the day. You offer advice and support. Visit someone who is ill or in need of help.

AUGUST 2013

Thursday, August 1 (Moon in Gemini)   The moon is in your ninth house today, the home of higher learning. You're full of ideas now on matters such as philosophy or religion, the law or publishing. You also have a strong interest in foreign travel or a foreign nation. It's a good time to look to the big picture. Break away from your routine or the usual way you think about things.

Friday, August 2 (Moon into Cancer, 11:30 p.m.) It's a number 5 day. Approach the day with an unconventional mindset. Release old structures; get a new point of view. Variety is the spice of life. Think freedom, no restrictions. Change and variety are highlighted now.

Saturday, August 3 (Moon in Cancer) The moon is in your tenth house today, and that means professional concerns take priority, even on a Saturday. Your life is more public. You gain an elevation in prestige. You're more responsive to the needs and moods of a group and the public in general. But don't blur the boundary between your personal and professional lives.

Sunday, August 4 (Moon in Cancer) It's all about your home, family, and personal environment. You're intuitive and nurturing, and home life is important to you. Tend to loved ones; do something with your children or sweetheart. Take time to maintain or beautify your home.

Monday, August 5 (Moon into Leo, 11:58 a.m.) It's a number 8 day, your power day, so focus on a power play, Libra. You can go far with your plans and achieve financial success. Open your mind to a new approach that could bring in big bucks. It's a good day to buy a lotto ticket.

Tuesday, August 6 (Moon in Leo) There's a new moon in your eleventh house today. That means new opportunities surface related to friends or a group of like-minded people. It's an ideal time to focus on your wishes and dreams. Examine your overall goals, and make sure that they remain an expression of who you are. With Uranus trine to the moon, you gain sudden insight, and your dreams are vivid.

Wednesday, August 7 (Moon into Virgo, 10:58 p.m.) You're at the top of your cycle today. Trust your hunches; intuition is highlighted. You're inventive and make connections that others overlook. You're determined and courageous. Stress originality. In romance something new is developing.

Thursday, August 8 (Moon in Virgo)   You probably feel like working behind the scenes today and staying out of public view. That's fine, but with Mercury moving into your eleventh house, you have a good opportunity to work with friends and a group. You can express your thoughts well and are understood, especially if you work for the common good.

Friday, August 9 (Moon in Virgo)   With the moon in your twelfth house today, you communicate your deepest feelings to another person. With others, it's still best to keep your feelings secret. Be aware that unconscious attitudes can be difficult now. So can relations with women. Follow your intuition, and look forward to meetings with friends and associates next week.

Saturday, August 10 (Moon into Libra, 8:09 a.m.)
It's a number 4 day, a good day to get organized. Clean out your garage, attic, or closet. Tear down the old in order to rebuild. Be methodical and thorough. Missing papers are found. Revise and rewrite. You're building a creative base.

Sunday, August 11 (Moon in Libra)   With the moon in your first house today, you get fired up, Libra, recharged for the month ahead. Your thoughts and emotions are aligned. You could be somewhat moody today, shifting from happy one moment, sad the next, then back again. You're dealing with your self-awareness, your appearance, and the person you are becoming.

Monday, August 12 (Moon into Scorpio, 3:19 p.m.)
It's a number 6 day. Focus on making people happy. Service to others is the theme of the day. You offer advice and support. Visit someone who is ill or in need of help.

Tuesday, August 13 (Moon in Scorpio)   The moon is in your second house today. Money and material goods are important to you now and give you a sense of security. You identify emotionally with your possessions or whatever you value. Watch your spending.

Wednesday, August 14 (Moon into Sagittarius, 8:05 p.m.)   Business discussions go well. You pull off a financial coup. It's your power day, your day to play it your way. Unexpected money arrives. It's a good day for buying a lottery ticket. Financial gain is at hand.

Thursday, August 15 (Moon in Sagittarius)   The moon is in your third house today. Take what you know, and share it with others. But stay in control of your emotions when communicating. You write from a deep place today; it's a good day for journaling, especially about matters from the past.

Friday, August 16 (Moon into Capricorn, 10:26 p.m.)
Venus moves into your first house today. You're physically vital, and relations with the opposite sex go well.

Your appearance and personality shine, and others find you appealing. Your feelings and thoughts are aligned. You're recharged for the rest of the month and beyond. Your face is in the public and attracting attention.

Saturday, August 17 (Moon in Capricorn)   The moon is in your fourth house today. Spend time with your family and other loved ones. Stick close to home if possible. You feel a close tie to your roots. You're dealing with the foundations of who you are and who you are becoming. A parent plays a role.

Sunday, August 18 (Moon into Aquarius, 11:07 p.m.)   It's a number 3 day. Take time to relax, enjoy yourself, recharge your batteries. Have fun today in preparation for tomorrow's discipline and focus. Remain flexible in your schedule today. Foster generosity.

Monday, August 19 (Moon in Aquarius)   With the moon in your fifth house, your emotions tend to overpower your intellect today. Be yourself; be emotionally honest. In love there's greater emotional depth to a relationship. You're also emotionally in touch with your creative side.

Tuesday, August 20 (Moon into Pisces, 11:44 p.m.) There's a full moon in your fifth house today, and that means yesterday's energy flows strongly into your Tuesday. You gain insight and illumination related to a creative endeavor. Children play a role in your day. You reap what you've sown.

Wednesday, August 21 (Moon in Pisces)   The moon is in your sixth house today. Don't let your fears hold you back. Help others, but don't deny your own needs. Visit someone who is ill, but don't forget about your own health needs. Keep up with your exercise plan, and watch your diet.

Thursday, August 22 (Moon in Pisces)   Your imagination is highlighted. Watch for psychic events, synchronicities. Universal knowledge, eternal truths, and deep spirituality are the themes of the day. You respond emotionally to whatever is happening now.

Friday, August 23 (Moon into Aries, 2:13 a.m.) It's a number 8 day. You can go far with your plans and achieve financial success, especially if you open your mind to a new approach. You're aggressive in seeking your goals, but keep in mind that you're playing with power, so be careful not to hurt others. Business discussions go well.

Saturday, August 24 (Moon in Aries)   The moon is in your seventh house today. You get along well with others. You can fit in just about anywhere. Loved ones and partners are more important than usual. You comprehend the nuances of a situation, but it's difficult to go with the flow. Be careful that others don't manipulate your feelings.

Sunday, August 25 (Moon into Taurus, 8:14 a.m.) It's a number 1 day, and you're at the top of your cycle again. You get a fresh start. Creativity is emphasized.

Don't be afraid to turn in a new direction. Get out and meet new people, have new experiences, do something you've never done before. In romance something new is developing.

Monday, August 26 (Moon in Taurus)   The moon is in your eighth house today. You pursue an interest in psychic power, the paranormal, the unknown. You wonder about the big issues, why you are here and what life is about. You might explore concepts of life after death and reincarnation. Intense feelings arise as you dig deep for answers.

Tuesday, August 27 (Moon into Gemini, 6:08 p.m.) Mars moves into your twelfth house today and stays there until October 15. You have a strong desire to work behind the scenes. Your thoughts and focus turn inward. However, be aware that an old issue you thought was buried boils to the surface, and you need to confront the matter head on.

Wednesday, August 28 (Moon in Gemini)   The moon is in your ninth house today, the home of higher learning. You're full of ideas now on matters such as philosophy or religion, the law or publishing. You also have a strong interest in foreign travel or a foreign nation. It's a good time to look to the big picture. Break away from your routine or the usual way you think about things.

Thursday, August 29 (Moon in Gemini)   You're talkative and mentally alert today, but you tend to analyze and rationalize too much. You're curious about what's going on, Libra, and looking for intellectual stimulation.

Friday, August 30 (Moon into Cancer, 6:33 a.m.) It's a number 6 day. It's a service day. Adjust to the needs of loved ones. You serve, teach, and guide. But know when to say enough is enough. Alternately, a change in the home, an adjustment or readjustment, is needed now. Don't put off the situation. That will only aggravate the problem.

Saturday, August 31 (Moon in Cancer) The moon is in your tenth house today, and that means professional concerns follow you into your Saturday. It's a good day for dealing with the public. You get an elevation of prestige that could include a raise, a bonus, or a commendation.

SEPTEMBER 2013

Sunday, September 1 (Moon into Leo, 7:02 p.m.) It's a number 5 day. You're versatile and changeable. It's a good time to promote new ideas and follow your curiosity. Freedom of thought and action is key. Think outside the box. Variety is the spice of life.

Monday, September 2 (Moon in Leo) The moon is in your eleventh house today. You might feel a need to withdraw and work behind the scenes, where you'll feel more grounded. Things concerning the past, even your childhood, play a role. It's best to hide your emotions and moodiness. Be aware that a secret enemy might have entered the mix.

Tuesday, September 3 (Moon in Leo)   You're at center stage today, Libra. You like to flaunt and celebrate. Be wild, imaginative; be the person you always imagined you might be. Play with different personae. Theatrics and drama are highlighted, perhaps involving children.

Wednesday, September 4 (Moon into Virgo, 5:45 a.m.)   It's a number 8 day, your power day, and your chance to make a financial leap. Open your mind to a new approach, but make sure that nothing you do is meant to harm others. Business dealings go well. However, you're playing with power, so be careful not to hurt others.

Thursday, September 5 (Moon in Virgo)   A new moon in your twelfth house brings opportunities related to your pursuit of a mystical or spiritual matter. Take time to meditate. You can easily expand your awareness today. Your intuition is heightened. Communicate your deepest feelings to someone close to you, but otherwise keep your feelings secret.

Friday, September 6 (Moon into Libra, 2:14 p.m.) Express your opinions dynamically. You attract creative people now. Stress originality. You're inspired to turn your career in a new direction. Don't fear change. Be bold and creative. Trust your hunches.

Saturday, September 7 (Moon in Libra) The moon is on your ascendant today. The way you see yourself now is the way others see you. Your appearance and personality shine. You're recharged for the rest of the month, and this makes you more appealing to the public. You're physically vital, and relations with the opposite sex go well.

Sunday, September 8 (Moon into Scorpio, 8:45 p.m.) You're creative and express yourself well today. Your artistic talents are highlighted. Enjoy the harmony, beauty, and pleasures of life. Overall, the social energy of the day is warm and welcoming. Spread your good news, and take time to listen to others.

Monday, September 9 (Moon in Scorpio) Yesterday's energy flows into your Monday. With Mercury moving into your first house, Libra, you communicate extremely well. You also adapt quickly and smoothly to changing circumstances. You're mentally restless and looking for new ideas.

Tuesday, September 10 (Moon in Scorpio) The moon is in your second house today. Money and material goods are important to you and give you a sense of security. You identify emotionally with your possessions or whatever you value. Expect emotional experiences related to money. Look at your priorities in handling your income.

Wednesday, September 11 (Moon into Sagittarius, 1:36 a.m.) Venus moves into your second house today. You celebrate your improved sense of affluence. A money-making scheme points you on a path toward freedom and flexibility. Money and material goods give you a sense of security.

Thursday, September 12 (Moon in Sagittarius) With the moon in your third house today, your mental abilities are strong, Libra, and you have an emotional need to reinvigorate your studies, especially regarding matters of the past. You're attracted to historical or archaeological studies. Take what you know, and share it, but don't expect others to be as excited as you are about delving into the past.

Friday, September 13 (Moon into Capricorn, 4:56 a.m.) It's a number 8 day, a good day to buy a lotto ticket. It's your power day, your day to play it your way. You can go far with your plans and achieve financial success. Unexpected money comes your way.

Saturday, September 14 (Moon in Capricorn) With the moon in your fourth house today, it's a good day to spend time with your family and other loved ones. Stick close to home. You're dealing with the foundations of who you are and who you are becoming. Retreat to a private place for meditation. See if you can remember your dreams from last night.

Sunday, September 15 (Moon into Aquarius, 7:06 a.m.) It's a number 1 day, and you're at the top of your cycle again. Be bold and creative. Trust your hunches; intuition is highlighted. Stress independence and originality in whatever actions you're taking or decisions you're making. In romance something new is developing

Monday, September 16 (Moon in Aquarius)   The moon is in your fifth house today. Be yourself; be emotionally honest. In love there's greater emotional depth to a relationship. You're emotionally in touch with your creative side. It's a good day to take a chance, experiment.

Tuesday, September 17 (Moon into Pisces, 8:59 a.m.) You're innovative and creative and communicate well. Your imagination is keen, and your popularity is on the rise. Your attitude determines everything today. Ease up on routines. Spread your good news.

Wednesday, September 18 (Moon in Pisces)   The moon is in your sixth house today. Keep your resolutions about exercise, and watch your diet. Attend to details related to your health. Make a doctor or dentist appointment. Help others, but don't deny your own needs.

Thursday, September 19 (Moon into Aries, 11:58 a.m.)   There's a full moon in your sixth house today. You reap what you've sown related to your daily work. It's a time of completion. Be of service to others, but don't limit yourself or let your fears hold you back. Get ready to move ahead, but take care of any health issues.

Friday, September 20 (Moon in Aries)   Pluto goes direct in your fourth house today, where it will remain until 2024. That releases more energy related to your home and domestic life. It's all about your roots and your heritage. The land or property you own or live on becomes more important. Keep in mind that Pluto transforms everything that is not needed.

Saturday, September 21 (Moon into Taurus, 5:34 p.m.) It's a number 7 day. You're setting out on a journey into the unknown to pursue a mystery. Be aware of intrigue and confidential information. Dig deep for answers, but don't make any absolute decisions until tomorrow. Stay emotionally balanced.

Sunday, September 22 (Moon in Taurus) The moon is in your eighth house of shared resources and investments today. Your experiences are more intense than usual. You have a strong sense of duty and feel obligated to fulfill your promises. Security is an important issue with you right now. It's a good day for dealing with mortgages, insurance, and investments.

Monday, September 23 (Moon in Taurus) You're feeling strong willed today. You could be somewhat stubborn, holding on to fixed opinions. Your senses are highly developed, and you're feeling more sensual than usual, Libra. While you maintain a common-sense, down-to-earth perspective on life, you also long for the good life with its material blessings.

Tuesday, September 24 (Moon into Gemini, 2:35 a.m.) It's a number 1 day, and you're at the top of your cycle again. Be bold and creative. Trust your hunches; intuition is highlighted. Stress independence and originality in whatever actions you're taking or decisions you're making. In romance something new is developing.

Wednesday, September 25 (Moon in Gemini) The moon is in your ninth house today. You're feeling as if you need to get away. Plan a trip, or sign up for a seminar or workshop. A foreign country or person of foreign birth could play a role.

Thursday, September 26 (Moon into Cancer, 2:25 p.m.) It's a number 3 day. Enjoy the harmony, beauty, and pleasures of life. Your attitude determines everything today. You're warm and receptive to what others say. You're curious and inventive. You communicate well.

Friday, September 27 (Moon in Cancer) The moon is in your tenth house today. You communicate well with coworkers, and Libra. You're bold and dramatic, but also more responsive to the needs of a group. It's a good day for sales and dealing with the public.

Saturday, September 28 (Moon in Cancer) You're especially intuitive today and also sensitive to other people's moods. So it's best to keep some things to yourself. Watch for meaningful coincidences to pop up. Get out and take a walk.

Sunday, September 29 (Moon into Leo, 2:58 a.m.) Mercury moves into your second house. There's a lot of talk now about finances, insurance, a mortgage, or credit cards. You enjoy networking and teaching. Your intellect is keen now, and you're focusing your mind on commerce. At the same time, you stick with your values.

Monday, September 30 (Moon in Leo)   The moon is in your eleventh house. Friends play an important role in your day, and you take the initiative to get together with them. You find strength in numbers and meaning through friends and groups. Gemini and Aquarius friends fit well with you now.

OCTOBER 2013

Tuesday, October 1 (Moon into Virgo, 1:53 p.m.) It's a number 6 day. Service to others is the theme of the day. You offer advice and support. Focus on making people happy. Be sympathetic, kind, and compassionate, but avoid scattering your energies. Be understanding, and avoid confrontations.

Wednesday, October 2 (Moon in Virgo)   The moon is in your twelfth house today. It's a great day for a mystical or spiritual discipline. Your intuition is heightened. Unconscious attitudes can be difficult now, so can relations with women. Think carefully before you act. There's a tendency to undo all the positive actions you've taken.

Thursday, October 3 (Moon into Libra, 10:00 p.m.) It's your power day, Libra. You attract financial success by starting something new. You're persuasive in business dealings that pay off in a big way. You can expand your horizons and gain recognition and power.

Friday, October 4 (Moon in Libra)   There's a new moon in your first house today. A doorway opens, and you gain a new sense of freedom. New opportunities arise related to something you did yesterday. But you're restless now and not sure what to do. You're malleable and open to change.

Saturday, October 5 (Moon in Libra)   The moon is on your ascendant. The way you see yourself now is the way others see you. You're physically vital, and relations with the opposite sex go well. Your thoughts and feelings are aligned.

Sunday, October 6 (Moon into Scorpio, 3:33 a.m.) It's a number 2 day. Partnerships are highlighted. Show your appreciation to others. Use your intuition to get a sense of your day. Don't make waves. Don't rush or show resentment; just let things develop.

Monday, October 7 (Moon in Scorpio)   Venus moves into your third house today. Educational opportunities come your way this month. You're especially interested in pursuing cultural and artistic endeavors, Libra. It's a good day for working on an enjoyable writing project. Your creativity is heightened. Music plays a role in your day. You get along well with family members, siblings, and neighbors.

Tuesday, October 8 (Moon into Sagittarius, 7:22 a.m.)   Your organizational skills are highlighted. Be methodical and thorough. Stay focused, and persevere to get things done. Emphasize quality. You're building foundations for an outlet for your creativity.

Wednesday, October 9 (Moon in Sagittarius) The moon is in your third house today. You're probably going from place to place taking care of your everyday needs. Get in touch with others, especially siblings, other relatives, or neighbors. You'll have some things to talk about, a message to pass on. Be careful while driving and talking on your cell. Your thinking may be unduly influenced by the past.

Thursday, October 10 (Moon into Capricorn, 10:18 a.m.) Service to others is the theme of the day, and diplomacy wins the way. Be sympathetic and kind, generous and tolerant. Domestic purchases are highlighted. The music is playing, so find your rhythm.

Friday, October 11 (Moon in Capricorn) The moon is in your fourth house today. Get organized now. You're dealing with foundations, the very foundations of who you are and who you are becoming. Make an effort to change a bad habit. It's best to work on your own. Stay focused, and don't let others distract you.

Saturday, October 12 (Moon into Aquarius, 1:00 p.m.) It's a number 8 day. It's your power day and your day to play it your way. A risk pays off. Expect a windfall. Try a new approach, and expect a financial gain. But remember that you're playing with power, so be careful not to hurt others.

Sunday, October 13 (Moon in Aquarius) The moon is in your fifth house today. You're emotionally in touch with your creative side. But be aware that your emotions tend to overpower your intellect. Be yourself; be emotionally honest. In love there's greater emotional depth to a relationship. You feel strongly attached to loved ones, particularly children.

Monday, October 14 (Moon into Pisces, 4:06 p.m.)
It's a number 1 day. You get a fresh start for the new month on this Monday. Take the lead on a project, and don't be afraid to turn in a new direction. Creativity is emphasized. In romance make room for a new love. A flirtation could turn serious.

Tuesday, October 15 (Moon in Pisces)   With Mars in your twelfth house today, your thoughts, desires, and actions are heavily influenced by unconscious motivations. That means that your deepest feelings surface and affect your thinking. It's best to release any anger you've been holding in. You tend to keep your plans secret now to avoid opposition. You feel best working on your own.

Wednesday, October 16 (Moon into Aries, 8:19 p.m.)
It's a number 3 day. You're innovative and creative and communicate well today. Enjoy the harmony, beauty, and pleasures of life. Your popularity is on the rise. Your imagination is keen now. Ease up on routines, and spread your good news.

Thursday, October 17 (Moon in Aries)   The moon is in your seventh house today. Partnerships are emphasized. You get along well with others. You can fit in just about anywhere, and you feel a need to be accepted. Loved ones are more important than usual.

Friday, October 18 (Moon in Aries)   There's a lunar eclipse in your seventh house today. Something that happens related to a partnership or contract creates a strong emotional impact. Any conflicts will be more emotional than usual, and you'll have a difficult time remaining detached and objective.

Saturday, October 19 (Moon into Taurus, 2:28 a.m.) It's a number 6 day. Diplomacy wins the way today. Do a good deed for someone. Visit someone who is ill or in need of help. Focus on making people happy. Be sympathetic, kind, and compassionate. Domestic purchases are highlighted.

Sunday, October 20 (Moon in Taurus)   The moon is in your eighth house today. Your experiences are more intense than usual. You have a strong sense of duty and feel obligated to fulfill your promises. Security is an important issue with you right now. You could find yourself managing or controlling someone else's assets.

Monday, October 21 (Moon into Gemini, 11:15 a.m.)   Mercury goes retrograde in your second house today and stays there until November 10. There could be some communication breakdown over the next three weeks regarding financial matters. There could be delays or glitches related to business travel plans. Expect some confusion or misinterpretation of what you say or write. Best not to sign contracts. If you must do so, read the small print.

Tuesday, October 22 (Moon in Gemini)   The moon is in your ninth house today. That means it's a good time to start thinking about a long trip. Make your plans now. You're feeling restless. It's also a good time to explore ideas, philosophies, mythology. You're a dreamer and thinker.

Wednesday, October 23 (Moon into Cancer, 10:37 p.m.) It's a number 1 day. You're at the top of your cycle. That means you get a fresh start, a new beginning. Don't be afraid to turn in a new direction. Trust your hunches. Express your opinions dynamically. Get out and meet new people, have new experiences, do something you've never done before.

Thursday, October 24 (Moon in Cancer) The moon is in your tenth house today. You're feeling ambitious, pushing ahead in your career. It's a good day for sales and dealing with the public. You've got your eye on a promotion. You're aiming high, shooting for the moon, so to speak.

Friday, October 25 (Moon in Cancer) You're sensitive to other people's moods today, Libra. It might seem as if those around you are turning against you. Don't worry; they are not. Take plenty of breaks from your work. Get out and take a walk. That will help you clear your head and improve your focus when you return to work. Best to keep your thoughts to yourself.

Saturday, October 26 (Moon into Leo, 11:13 a.m.) It's a number 4 day. Hard work is called for. You make use of your organizational skills. Be methodical and thorough. Persevere to get things done. You're building foundations, establishing a creative base. Romance goes to the back burner for now.

Sunday, October 27 (Moon in Leo)   The moon is in your eleventh house today. You work well with others, especially in a group. Friends play a surprisingly important role, notably Gemini and Aquarius. Focus on your wishes and dreams. Examine your overall goals, and make sure that they're still an expression of who you are.

Monday, October 28 (Moon into Virgo, 10:45 p.m.) It's a number 6 day. Service to others is the theme of the day, and diplomacy wins the way. Be sympathetic and kind, generous and tolerant. Domestic purchases are highlighted. The music is playing, so find your rhythm.

Tuesday, October 29 (Moon in Virgo)   The moon is in your twelfth house today. You may feel a need to withdraw and work behind the scenes. Think carefully before you act. There's a tendency now to undo all the positive actions you've take. Avoid any self-destructive behavior. Be aware of hidden enemies.

Wednesday, October 30 (Moon in Virgo)   You might find that your colleagues are speeding ahead of you while you are stuck checking details on your project. Take your time and proceed at your own pace, and don't let the pace of others intimidate you. Alternately, tend to any health-related matters. Exercise, and watch your diet. Stop worrying and fretting.

Thursday, October 31 (Moon into Libra, 7:22 a.m.)
It's all about beginnings and endings today. Accept what comes your way. It's all part of a cycle. Use the day for reflection, expansion, and concluding projects. Get ready for something new, but don't start anything yet.

NOVEMBER 2013

Friday, November 1 (Moon in Libra)   It's all about your health and your emotional self: how you feel and how you feel about yourself. You're dealing with the person you are becoming. You tend to search for ways to improve yourself, and you focus on how the public relates to you. It's difficult to remain detached and objective now. Your feelings tend to fluctuate by the moment. Try not to procrastinate or change your plans.

Saturday, November 2 (Moon into Scorpio, 1:35 p.m.)   It's a number 8 day, your power day. Business discussions go well. You attract financial success. Open your mind to a new approach that could bring in big bucks. You have a chance to expand, to gain recognition, even fame and power.

Sunday, November 3—Daylight Saving Time Ends (Moon in Scorpio)   There's a solar eclipse in your second house today. That means new opportunities come your way related to your finances. With four planets also in Scorpio, everything is enhanced—for better or worse—especially issues related to money and material things. It's the beginning or end of something that could be related to changes in your ideals or whatever you value.

Monday, November 4 (Moon into Sagittarius, 3:14 p.m.)   It's a number 1 day, and you're at the top of your cycle. You take the lead in something new and get a fresh start, a new beginning. Stress originality. You attract creative people and avoid those with closed minds. Trust your hunches.

Tuesday, November 5 (Moon in Sagittarius)   Venus moves into your fourth house today. You're very happy with your home life this month. The domestic scene is serene and filled with love. You could be working on a project to renovate and beautify your home. It's a labor of love and done with many artistic touches.

Wednesday, November 6 (Moon into Capricorn, 4:44 p.m.)   Your attitude determines everything today, Libra. You keep everyone in balance around you. Spread your good news, and take time to listen to others. Ease up on routines. Your charm and wit are appreciated. You're innovative and creative and communicate well.

Thursday, November 7 (Moon in Capricorn)   Jupiter goes direct in your tenth house today. That's good news. Now you have an opportunity to expand your career goals. You see the big picture. You could gain an elevation of prestige, a raise, a bonus, or a commendation.

Friday, November 8 (Moon into Aquarius, 6:31 p.m.)   It's a number 4 day and time to get focused. Your organizational skills are highlighted. Emphasize quality as you fulfill your obligations. Persevere to get things done today. Revise and rewrite. You're building foundations for an outlet for your creativity. However, it's not a day for experimentation or new approaches.

Saturday, November 9 (Moon in Aquarius)   With the moon in your fifth house today, you're feeling a sudden surge of inspiration, a creative urge that helps you break through a block. In romance there's more depth and understanding in a relationship. Children play an important role in your day.

Sunday, November 10 (Moon into Pisces, 9:37 p.m.) Mercury goes direct in your second house today. Any confusion or miscommunication that you've been experiencing, especially related to finances, recedes into the past. Things move more smoothly now. You get your ideas across. Others understand your ideals or what you value.

Monday, November 11 (Moon in Pisces)   The moon is in your sixth house today. You enjoy your work now and get along with fellow workers. The work environment is harmonious, and you keep everyone in balance, Libra. Be careful not to overlook any seemingly minor matters that could take on importance. Keep up with your exercise plan, and watch your diet.

Tuesday, November 12 (Moon in Pisces) Ideas are ripe today. You can tap deeply into the collective unconscious for inspiration. Keep track of your dreams, including your daydreams. Your imagination is strong; you have a vivid fantasy life. You respond emotionally to whatever is happening now. You're inspired to turn your career in a new direction that benefits others as well as yourself.

Wednesday, November 13 (Moon into Aries, 2:40 a.m.) Neptune goes direct in your sixth house today. There could be some difficulties related to the workplace. Something secretive and deceptive is going on. Move with care when discussing your concerns. You face delays in your efforts to guide and help coworkers. Alternately, you could face some confusion related to a health issue.

Thursday, November 14 (Moon in Aries) The moon is in your seventh house today. Relationships take on more importance. You comprehend the nuances of a situation, but it's difficult to go with the flow. You might have trouble now getting in touch with your own feelings. Alternately, a legal matter comes to your attention.

Friday, November 15 (Moon into Taurus, 9:50 a.m.) It's a number 3 day. Intuition is highlighted. Spread your good news, and take time to listen to others. You can influence people with your upbeat attitude. Have fun today in preparation for tomorrow's discipline and focus.

Saturday, November 16 (Moon in Taurus) With the moon in your eighth house today, your experiences are more intense than usual. You have a strong sense of duty and feel obligated to fulfill your promises. You could be getting involved in managing or controlling someone's assets. Security is an important issue with you right now. Alternately, it's a good time to help out in a cause aimed at improving living conditions for large numbers of people.

Sunday, November 17 (Moon into Gemini, 7:08 p.m.) There's a full moon in your eighth house today. You gain insight and illumination related to matters such as insurance, credit cards, taxes, or inheritance. You reap what you've sown. It's a time of completion.

Monday, November 18 (Moon in Gemini) The moon is in your ninth house today. You may feel a need to get away now, a break from the usual routine, Libra. Visit a museum exhibit or art gallery opening. Pursue a new idea. Are you ready to plan a long trip or sign up for a seminar?

Tuesday, November 19 (Moon in Gemini) You see two sides of a situation, Libra. You try to keep everyone in balance. You're feeling restless and sending text messages or e-mail or making phone calls. It's a good time to write and revise. Your mind is quick today. You might be completing tasks faster than others, and they could have trouble keeping up with you.

Wednesday, November 20 (Moon into Cancer, 6:24 a.m.) It's a number 8 day, your power day. Business discussions go well. You attract financial success. Open your mind to a new approach that could bring in big bucks. You have a chance to expand, to gain recognition, even fame and power.

Thursday, November 21 (Moon in Cancer)   With the moon in your tenth house today, there's lots of activity now in your professional life. You love what you do and communicate well. You feel very emotional about your work or your fellow workers. You're in the public eye and gain a boost in prestige.

Friday, November 22 (Moon into Leo, 6:57 p.m.) It's a number 1 day, and you're at the top of your cycle. You take the lead in something new and get a fresh start, a new beginning. Stress originality. You attract creative people and avoid people with closed minds. Trust your hunches.

Saturday, November 23 (Moon in Leo)   The moon is in your eleventh house today, Libra. You work well with others, especially in a group. Friends play a surprisingly important role, especially Gemini and Libra. Focus on your wishes and dreams. Examine your overall goals, and make sure that they're still an expression of who you are.

Sunday, November 24 (Moon in Leo)   You're at center stage, Libra. It's a great day for promoting and publicizing yourself. Dress boldly; showmanship is emphasized. Be wild, imaginative; be the person you always imagined you might be. Play with different personae. Drama is highlighted, perhaps involving children.

Monday, November 25 (Moon into Virgo, 7:11 a.m.)
It's a number 4 day. Your organizational skills are highlighted. Persevere to get things done today. Don't get sloppy; be methodical and thorough. Tear down the old in order to rebuild. Keep your goals in mind; follow your ideas. Be tenacious; be persistent.

Tuesday, November 26 (Moon in Virgo) The moon is in your twelfth house today. Unconscious attitudes can be difficult, Libra. Keep your feelings secret. You might feel a need to withdraw and work on your own. You're good at keeping everyone in balance, but now you need to work on your own balance. Take time to reflect and meditate. It's a great time for pursuing a spiritual discipline.

Wednesday, November 27 (Moon into Libra, 5:00 p.m.) It's a service day, Libra. A domestic adjustment works out for the best. You could face emotional outbursts by someone making unfair demands. Be understanding, and avoid confrontations. Diplomacy wins the way. Help others, but dance to your own tune.

Thursday, November 28 (Moon in Libra) The moon is on your ascendant today. Your face is before the public and all over Facebook. You're recharged for the month ahead, and this makes you more appealing to the public. You're physically vital, and relations with the opposite sex go well. Your appearance and personality shine. Your feelings and thoughts are aligned. Happy Thanksgiving.

Friday, November 29 (Moon into Scorpio, 11:04 p.m.)   It's a number 8 day, another power day. You're ambitious and goal oriented. Remain confident and convinced that material success is within reach, if not already here. You're playing with power, so be careful not to hurt others.

Saturday, November 30 (Moon in Scorpio)   With the moon in your second house, you could gain a financial boost that feels like a jolt of energy. While that will make you feel more secure, you need to decide what your priorities are in handling your income. Temper your spending for now, even if you've just received an increase in your finances.

DECEMBER 2013

Sunday, December 1 (Moon in Scorpio)   You can expect intense, emotional experiences today. You're passionate about whatever you're doing. Your sexuality is heightened. Investigate, research, dig deep. Be aware of things happening in secret and possible deception. It's best to forgive and forget and try to avoid going to extremes.

Monday, December 2 (Moon into Sagittarius, 1:32 a.m.)   There's a new moon in your third house. New opportunities come your way related to a matter from the past. It could involve something in your community or neighborhood. You have much to say about the matter, but make sure you control your emotions. Be careful driving and talking on your cell phone.

Tuesday, December 3 (Moon in Sagittarius)   The moon is in your third house today. Your mental abilities are strong, and you have an emotional need to reinvigorate your studies, especially regarding matters of the past. You're attracted to historical studies or prehistorical explorations. Take what you know, and share it with others. You could be getting involved in a challenging mental activity, such as on-line gaming, a debate, or a game of chess.

Wednesday, December 4 (Moon into Capricorn, 1:51 a.m.)   With Mercury moving into your third house today, yesterday's energy flows into your Wednesday, is strengthened, and stays with you for the rest of the year and into January. You are more adaptable and versatile now. Your mind is active and busy. It's a good time to try out different possibilities. You express yourself well and get your ideas across.

Thursday, December 5 (Moon in Capricorn)   The moon is in your fourth house. You're dealing with your home life and the foundations of who you are. Spend time at home with family and other loved ones. Take the day off, if possible, or work at home. It's a good day to handle repairs on your house. Spend some time in meditation.

Friday, December 6 (Moon into Aquarius, 1:55 a.m.) Even though it's Friday, hard work and persistence are called for in order to get ahead. Make use of your organizational skills. Be methodical and thorough, and stay on task. You're building a base for your future. Be aware that you could feel overworked, but the weekend is near.

Saturday, December 7 (Moon in Aquarius)   With Mars moving into your first house today, you are active and energetic and feeling independent. You respond quickly and forcefully to changing circumstances. Some might find you a bit aggressive and overly assertive this month and into the new year. You're willing and able to start new projects now, but you might need to put more effort into following through with what you've begun.

Sunday, December 8 (Moon into Pisces, 3:35 a.m.) Domestic purchases are highlighted. Focus on making people happy. Do a good deed. It's a service day, so direct your energy toward helping others, Libra. Be generous and tolerant, even if it goes against your nature.

Monday, December 9 (Moon in Pisces)   The moon is in your sixth house today. Continue your good deeds from yesterday. Even though it's a Monday, you'll be upbeat and make the day better for everyone you meet.

Tuesday, December 10 (Moon into Aries, 8:06 a.m.) It's a number 8 day, your power day. It's your opportunity to expand and grow. Be courageous. You're playing with power, so be careful not to hurt others. Be aware that others in power may be watching your moves.

Wednesday, December 11 (Moon in Aries)   With the moon in your seventh house today, Libra, you turn your focus to partnerships, both business and personal. A legal matter could come to your attention. It's difficult to remain detached and objective. Women play a prominent role. Be careful that others don't manipulate your feelings.

Thursday, December 12 (Moon into Taurus, 3:41 p.m.) It's a number 1 day. Take the initiative to start something new. Individuality is stressed. You can turn in a new direction. Get out and meet new people, make new contacts. Make room for a new romance, if you're ready for it.

Friday, December 13 (Moon in Taurus) With the moon in your eighth house, Libra, you could attract powerful people to you today. Your energy is more intense than usual, and drama plays a role. Your emotions could affect your feelings about belongings that you share with others. An interest in metaphysics or related rituals grabs your attention.

Saturday, December 14 (Moon in Taurus) You can be somewhat stubborn now, particularly on your opinions about health issues and physical activity. You're highly sensual. It's a good day to cultivate ideas, especially related to money matters. You might profit from the purchase or sale of a property.

Sunday, December 15 (Moon into Gemini, 1:41 a.m.) It's a number 4 day. Control your impulses. Fulfill your obligations. Persevere to get things done today. Emphasize quality. You're building foundations for an outlet for your creativity.

Monday, December 16 (Moon in Gemini)   The moon is in your ninth house today. You're feeling as if you need to break out of your usual routine, or it could turn into a rut, Libra. Travel or higher education plays a role. Plan a trip or sign up for a seminar or workshop. A foreign country or person of foreign birth could play a role.

Tuesday, December 17 (Moon into Cancer, 1:17 p.m.) With Uranus going direct in your seventh house today, you feel a strong need to focus on partnerships and contracts. Just make sure that you make your plans or actions known to your partner, either personal or business. There's also a full moon in your ninth house, which suggests that you reap what you've sown or get a new perspective regarding higher education or long-distance travel. Take time to reflect on your interest in a foreign country or a person of foreign birth.

Wednesday, December 18 (Moon in Cancer)   The moon is in your tenth house today. Your tenacity is recognized. You gain an elevation in prestige related to your profession and career. Material success and financial security play a role in your day. You make a strong emotional commitment now to your profession or to a role in public life.

Thursday, December 19 (Moon in Cancer)   You're intuitive and nurturing now. Your home life is important to you. You could feel emotional today and overly sensitive to other people's moods. Best to keep your thoughts and criticisms to yourself. Get out and take a walk. Beautify your home.

Friday, December 20 (Moon into Leo, 1:48 a.m.)
It's a number 9 day. That means it's time to complete
a project. Clear your desk, and make room for the
new, but don't start anything until tomorrow. Spend
some time in deep thought. Consider how you can expand your base.

Saturday, December 21 (Moon in Leo)   Venus
goes retrograde in your fourth house today and stays
there until January 31. Plans related to changes in
your home life are interrupted or delayed. You might
become somewhat disgruntled about matters related
to someone in your home. You could have problems
getting along and general disagreements over the next
month. You also might have second thoughts later
about any contracts you sign during this time. A project to renovate or beautify your home could face delays.

Sunday, December 22 (Moon into Virgo, 2:20 p.m.)
It's a number 2 day. Cooperation is highlighted. Use
your intuition to get a sense of your day. Be kind and
understanding. Show your appreciation to others.
There could be some soul searching related to relationships.

Monday, December 23 (Moon in Virgo)   The
moon is in your twelfth house today. Think carefully
before you act. There's a tendency now to undo all the
positive actions you've taken. Avoid any self-
destructive behavior. It's best to work behind the
scenes and stay out of the public view. Be aware of
hidden enemies.

Tuesday, December 24 (Moon in Virgo)   Mercury moves into your fourth house today. There's lots of mental activity in the home now. Home schooling or games requiring mental skills are a possibility at this time. It could also mean that things are changing in the home, and you need to make adjustments.

Wednesday, December 25 (Moon into Libra, 1:18 a.m.)   It's a number 5 day. Approach the day with an unconventional mindset. Release old structures; get a new point of view. Freedom of thought and action is key. But so is moderation; avoid excess in whatever you're doing. Merry Christmas.

Thursday, December 26 (Moon in Libra)   The moon is in your first house today. Your self-awareness and appearance are important now. You're dealing with your emotional self, the person you are becoming. You might feel moody now—happy one moment, sad or withdrawn the next. However, your thoughts and feelings are aligned.

Friday, December 27 (Moon into Scorpio, 8:59 a.m.) You journey into the unknown today and investigate something hidden that's going on behind the scenes. You dig deep. You're exploring a mystery. Knowledge is essential to your success.

Saturday, December 28 (Moon in Scorpio)   With the moon in your second house, money issues surface. You could get a quick financial boost today. It's a good time for investments. Look at your priorities in spending your income. Take care of payments and collections.

Sunday, December 29 (Moon into Sagittarius, 12:38 p.m.) Finish the year by wrapping up a project and preparing for something new. Take time to reflect on everything that's been going on. Look for a way to expand your horizons, but don't start anything until the new year.

Monday, December 30 (Moon in Sagittarius) The moon is in your third house today. You're busy interacting with neighbors, relatives, or siblings in a social gathering. You get your ideas across, but try not to get too emotional. A female relative plays an important role.

Tuesday, December 31 (Moon into Capricorn, 1:02 p.m.) It's a number 2 day. Cooperation and partnerships are highlighted. You're diplomatic and capable of fixing whatever has gone wrong. As usual, you're concerned about keeping everything in balance, Libra. That's your native energy. You excel in working with a group now. You're playing the role of the visionary today. Be honest and open. Enjoy your New Year's Eve. Everything in moderation is the theme.

HAPPY NEW YEAR!

SYDNEY OMARR

Born on August 5, 1926, in Philadelphia, Pennsylvania, **Sydney Omarr** was the only person ever given full-time duty in the U.S. Army as an astrologer. He is regarded as the most erudite astrologer of the twentieth century and the best known, through his syndicated column and his radio and television programs (he was Merv Griffin's "resident astrologer"). Omarr has been called the most "knowledgeable astrologer since Evangeline Adams." His forecasts of Nixon's downfall, the end of World War II in mid-August of 1945, the assassination of John F. Kennedy, Roosevelt's election to a fourth term and his death in office ... these and many others are on the record and quoted enough to be considered "legendary."

ABOUT THE SERIES

This is one of a series of twelve *Sydney Omarr®
Day-by-Day Astrological Guides* for the signs of
2013. For questions and comments about the
book, go to www.sydneyomarr.blogspot.com.

SIGNET

COMING SOON

SYDNEY OMARR'S® ASTROLOGICAL GUIDE FOR YOU IN 2013

As we begin the new year, these expert forecasts for 2013 offer valuable insights about the past and extraordinary predictions for the future. Brimming with tantalizing projections, this amazing guide will give you advice on romantic commitment, career moves, travel, and finance. Along with year overviews and detailed month-by-month predictions for every sign, you'll learn everything that's new under the stars, including:

- What to expect from relationships with family and partners
- New career opportunities for success in the future
- Global shifts and world forecasts
- And much more!

Available wherever books are sold or at penguin.com